CW01512564

Carl-Auer

Jakob Robert Schneider

Family Constellations

Basic Principles and Procedures

Translated by Colleen Beaumont

2007

© 2007 Carl-Auer-Systeme Verlag, Heidelberg. All rights reserved.
No part of the book may be reproduced by any process whatsoever
without the written permission of the copyright owner.
Title of the original edition: "Das Familienstellen"
© 2006, Carl-Auer Systeme Verlag, Heidelberg

DTP: Drißner-Design u. DTP, Meßstetten
Cover: WSP-Design, Heidelberg
Coverpainting: Maja Rodrian, Munich
Printed in the Netherlands
Koninklijke Wöhrmann, Zutphen

ISBN 978-3-89670-594-5

Bibliografic information published by Die Deutsche Nationalbibliothek
Die Deutsche Nationalbibliothek lists this publication
in the Deutsche Nationalbibliografie; detailed bibliografic
data available on Internet http://dnb.ddb.de.

Carl-Auer Verlag
Häusserstraße 14
69115 Heidelberg
Germany
www.carl-auer.com

Table of Contents

Foreword

This book does not actually need a foreword, nor does it need any words of invitation, preparation, or explanation. It speaks entirely for itself. Originally, the book was planned as a compact introduction to family constellation work and was to be part of a new series of introductions to various systemic approaches and related topics. The task of streamlining shortening a manuscript makes it pithier, more lively and forceful. As we read Jakob Schneider's first draft, however, it was clear that it was already so clear and compact that it would be a pity to cut it shorter, so we encouraged him to do the opposite and expand the text.

The result is a completely up-to-date, basic introduction to family constellations that is well structured, concise, and supported by many clear and often touching case examples. It summarises the development, basic principles, focus, attitude, and procedures of constellations and it does so in a way that is always logical, differentiated, and stimulating. To round it off, there are a few basic theoretical considerations.

All of the insights, concepts, principles, and basics that were initially developed by Bert Hellinger (conscience, soul, orders of love and helping, dynamics of bonds and entanglements, and resolution), are included here in brief, in a form that is easy to understand. I know of no book that describes the broad scope of family constellations in such a clear, compact, yet comprehensive way. This book does not preach, it does not seduce, and it does not immobilise. Rather, it invites readers to form their own ideas about family constellations and to draw their own conclusions. In the author's style and expression, readers already have a taste of the attitude that underlies all family constellation work: collected awareness, a respectful orientation towards resources and resolutions, and extreme reserve in setting intentions or goals.

Jakob Schneider has been friends with Bert Hellinger for many years and is the only therapist who has continued long-term to offer constellation work the way Bert Hellinger developed it. Because of his non-dogmatic, non-prescriptive, neutral stance, readers are not tempted to react to the ideas defensively as has happened (at least to me) with other books on family constellations. Although Jakob Schneider remains very close to Bert Hellinger's conceptualisation, this book is very much his own. Constellation work has been at the centre of his work and that of his wife, Sieglinde, for a very long time, and his intensive confrontation with the work through twenty years of experience is clearly visible. The work is clearly embodied in him in his flesh and blood (or, perhaps the work is individually "tailored" to him, in keeping with his name, Schneider, the German word for tailor). Since he often works abroad, the book opens a wide horizon that often goes far beyond the usual boundaries of counselling and psychotherapy in a sensitive way that I find satisfying and not artificially elevated.

Just as Paul Watzlawick was able to present Gregory Bateson's ideas to readers in an attractive and accessible way, this book could help to raise awareness of Bert Hellinger's insights and of family constellation work, a work whose deep and unique effects continue to move and amaze me.

The book has something to offer everyone who is already working with constellations, but also those who are interested in gaining an overview of this work.

Gunthard Weber
Wiesloch, February 2007

Prologue

The family constellation work initiated by Bert Hellinger has now grown far beyond its infancy. In an astoundingly short period of time, the work has spread to reach large numbers of people in German-speaking countries and further throughout the world. The people attracted to this approach are interested in problem-solving methods that also incorporate an awareness of the existence of the human soul. Many psychotherapists and counsellors from various backgrounds are now offering constellation work in a wide range of therapeutic settings with groups, individuals, couples, and families.

Alongside the spread of family constellations and other systemic constellation work, there has been widespread criticism voiced about Bert Hellinger and other constellation leaders, and about the method in general. Unfortunately, the criticism has too often been put forth without any basis in actual experience or an in-depth knowledge of what really happens in family constellations.

So, what really happens in family constellations? What insights and experiences are engendered by this "phenomenological-systemic" method, as it is sometimes called? What does one need to know in order to understand family constellations, or to practise the method? What is needed to understand the basic methodology, the processes of bonding and resolution in a relationship system, the role of conscience, the soul, fate, entanglements and the kind of acceptance that bring resolution? How strongly do the "orders of love" influence chances of success in a relationship? How do "orders" and "movements of the soul" fit together in constellations? In which areas of counselling and psychotherapy can family constellations be used, and what are the effects? In what sense can we understand the process in family constellations as phenomenological and systemic? What explanations can we offer for the fact that representatives seem to have access to a foreign sensory awareness, a key factor in the constellation method?

This book is intended for everyone who is interested in family constellations as well as those who are learning to use the method. It presents insights gleaned from 20 years' practice of family constellations that add to our general understanding of family dynamics and intimate human relationships. Those who are interested in delving deeper into the literature of family and systemic constellations are referred to the reading list, which includes books by Bert Hellinger and others.

There are few references to other literature and little discussion of a general nature in this book. It is restricted to a description of one method, and the basic processes of bonding and resolution in the soul as they appear in family constellations. I am writing from my own point of view, describing my own experiences and thoughts on the subject. It is not my intention to refute the wider criticisms of this method, nor to give an overview of the wide variety of methods and perspectives within the constellation work as a whole. Whenever any new method develops and spreads, there is a confrontation with other approaches and the emergence of new practices and applications. Starting with Bert Hellinger's original formulation, I hope to articulate a current understanding of constellation work that addresses the essentials of this approach, and also explores further implications, suggested by our experiences in constellations, as to the nature of relationships in our lives.

Throughout the book I have employed several linguistic conventions. When I refer simply to "the father" or "the mother", in the examples of constellations, I mean the representatives of these family members. If I am talking about the actual client or actual family members, I will make that clear. The case examples are largely related from memory and have been altered slightly to protect the anonymity of those involved. They are not intended to serve as documentation or "proof", but rather to illustrate particular concepts, and are accurate in all details relative to those concepts.

To avoid repeatedly mentioning that constellation leaders may be psychotherapists, counsellors, social workers, or others in the helping professions, I am using the word "therapist" for all those who lead constellations, and the word "client" for those who are seeking help or guidance. This presents some inherent problems, since family constellations, in and of themselves, are not psychotherapy, and those who are seeking help, guidance, or a path of personal development using this method are not necessarily in treatment of any kind. However, these terms seem to be the most comprehensive and understandable both for psychotherapists and for lay readers, and they reflect a general idea in the simplest way. I would ask the reader to take these terms only in the widest sense. This does not take into consideration any legal restrictions on who is allowed to practise psychotherapy or call themselves psychotherapists, or the various conditions under which constellation work may be offered. Those are separate regulatory issues, which are of practical importance.

A word about me, personally: I have been working with family constellations for twenty years. Following a constellation of my own family, led by Bert Hellinger in the early stages of his developing this method, I felt I had to try it out myself, immediately, in my work with youths and students. Family constellation work quickly became an invaluable core of my work as a marriage and family counsellor. My experiences as a friend of Bert Hellinger, and intense observer of his methods of working with clients and his style of teaching have furthered my own development and been adapted to suit my own personal style. Through constellation work, I have been privileged to meet many colleagues in Germany and abroad, and I continue to be impressed by the warm-hearted dedication, the depth of understanding, and the wide variety of personal expression that they have contributed to the development of family constellation work and to practices in their own areas. Without those meetings, this book would surely never have been written.

Countless clients have allowed me the privilege of participating in their fate and their exploration of change. Their contributions are also essential to this book, and I feel deeply connected to all of them.

I would like to give particular thanks to my friend, Dr Gunthard Weber, who prompted me to write the book. It is always a pleasure and a thrill to exchange ideas with him about family constellation. Thanks also to Dr Norbert Linz and Harald Scheubner for their editorial efforts and many valuable suggestions. My wife has played a very special role in the writing of this book. Her ear was always available for my many questions, her encouragement never wavered, and her profound understanding of the subject matter has greatly enriched my efforts.

This book is dedicated to my teacher and friend, Bert Hellinger. What he has opened up for me and so many others with his insights and his open heart is a great treasure.

For those of you who are already familiar with this subject, and those of you who are interested in learning something about it, I hope that this summarised presentation provides you a useful overview.

Jakob Robert Schneider
Munich, January 2007

1 Introduction
What is new and compelling about family constellations?

Those drawn to family constellations often look first at one person, Bert Hellinger. Many people have experienced him as helpful when they were in need, and have sensed in him a quality of strength and wisdom, a deep sensitivity towards the dynamics and degree of order in relationships, and an awareness of the soul's response to events. Therapists as well as clients have experienced a clear inner resonance and response to Hellinger and his work and a sense that what is transmitted rings true and is of great value. He has been intrepid in plumbing the depths of human fates, and has had the courage to openly reveal the potential and the limitations of his interventions.

However, Bert Hellinger's personal effectiveness alone does not adequately explain the rapid spread of family constellations. Whether in individual or group sessions, various elements of many psychotherapeutic approaches come together to create a tool that allows processes of the soul to be seen and experienced directly. It is a method that focuses on the factors that are essential for resolution. At the same time, this instrument leads into a depth of human experience and discovery that reaches beyond the sometimes-narrow boundaries of psychotherapy into an encompassing, collective realm of mind and spirit. Constellations reveal bonds in the soul that are related to events and fates within a family and larger groups, and they often lead to the resolution of the attendant difficulties.

Central to family constellation work is the concept of 'entanglement'. There may be a powerful impact in a constellation when we become aware that some of the pain we are suffering actually belongs to someone else in the past, but has not yet been laid to rest. We are not responding to actual experiences in our own lives; we seem to be trying to be of service to those in the past, attempting to bring peace to their souls.

Conflicts arise in the soul when opposing forces divide us internally or in our relationships to others. We are forced to either repress one side or engage in battle. We experience ourselves as divided and torn, indecisive and dissatisfied, under a strain that may even feel like insanity. Counselling or psychotherapy is the work of reconciling these warring factions. One of the primary attraction of constellation work is its power to reunite and reconcile such divisions.

This work makes clear that everyone, alive or dead, has an equal right to their place and connection to the system, regardless of their particular fate in life. It can support reconciliation between victims and perpetrators and their families and descendents, even in the most difficult of situations. Those who have been excluded from a family can be returned to their rightful places. Constellations offer a path that leads to peace in the heart, even in the throes of conflict.

An Example: Fear of Public Speaking

In an advanced training group for psychotherapists, a client was brought in to participate in a demonstration of family constellation work. The man stated his issue:

"I am at the top management level of my company and I often have to give presentations to large groups. Even though I am successful and respected in my work, I suffer from severe anxiety whenever I am doing a presentation in front of a group. Probably no one else notices it, but I always break out in a cold sweat. Sometimes the anxiety is so overwhelming that I try to get out of my obligations to give presentations." When asked to be more precise about his fears, he said that he couldn't say exactly what he was afraid of, but experienced a vague fear that something terrible could happen. He could not remember any personal experience that could logically account for his anxiety.

This middle aged, good-looking man was happily married and had two young children. His father had already died, but the man had had a good relationship with both of his parents. In an attempt to deal with his anxieties, the man had tried psychotherapy for a period of some months. Although the client-centred therapy was a positive experience, it did not relieve the presenting problem, which is what brought him to our group.

When asked about any significant events in his family of origin, the man could not immediately come up with any information that might be relevant. Since it was apparent that he was suffering greatly from this affliction, we proceeded with a constellation anyway, and asked him to choose representatives for his father, his mother and for himself, and place them in accordance with his inner sense of their relationship. He placed the father and his own representative facing each other but at a distance. He placed his mother somewhat off to the side, turned towards his father. The father immediately looked down at the floor and seemed very far away, with no relationship to his wife or son. As this sometimes suggests a death, I asked about his father's parents. The man explained, "My grandfather died very young, while my father was still a small child. My grandmother raised the children alone." The client was asked to place a representative for his grandfather next to his father. The father, without glancing up, moved several steps away and turned towards a window. The grandfather stood motionless for a while, looking at his grandson. The grandson (the client's representative) appeared shaky, and seemed mesmerised by his grandfather. The grandfather then made a curious gesture. Several times, he wiped his hands over his face and threw his head backwards. When asked what he was doing, he responded: "I don't know. It's as if something flew into my eyes and almost blew my head off."

The client was extremely moved and said: "My father never spoke about his own father, but my mother told me that before the war, my grandfather was a training officer in the army. One day he was demonstrating how to arm a hand grenade and the grenade exploded in his hand and killed him." No sooner had the man finished telling this story about his grandfather than, in the constellation, his father threw himself into the grandfather's arms with heart-wrenching sobs. As if floodgates had opened, all the deep pain and consequences of the terrible, gory past were released, presumably having been locked up in the father's family all this time. And we could see a strange parallel to the client's fears about something terrible happening during a presentation. Something terrible really had happened to his grandfather while giving a presentation to his troops. I asked the client to take his representative's place in the constellation and to approach his father and grandfather. The three men embraced warmly. There was a palpable feeling of relief in the entire training group, and the client appeared very relaxed at the end of the constellation.

This is just one of countless examples of what makes constellations so compelling to so many people. In a short period of time, something was revealed that was immediately understandable and touched the heart. It shed light on current personal difficulties and revealed connections between crucial events and relationships. It opened the possibility for resolution of the issues as well.

2 Constellation Processes

The idea of using strangers to represent personal process and relationships is not a new one. Very early on in psychodrama, JL Moreno used role-playing methods taken from improvisational theatre and made inner conflicts and relationship issues visible through dramatisation. Role-playing has also been a favoured method for sorting out social processes, using not only words, but also positioning and gestures. Virginia Satir had a finely tuned sensitivity to the network of family interactions and their effects on individual family members and in her family reconstructions, she created impressively staged scenes of entire multi-generational, extended families. Through the various dialogues that ensued, she would then track the family stories, almost like a detective, searching with her clients for clarification and understanding. "Sculpture" also allowed a glimpse into inner conflicts, as parts of an individual personality were portrayed and then rearranged to bring about useful movements.

Bert Hellinger intuitively grasped the importance of order in families in these psychotherapeutic methods and recognised that insight and direct experience were the essential goals of therapeutic intervention. He incorporated the use of representatives and intensified the process in his own style. He soon recognised that constellations offered a potential for portraying inner processes and the bonds of family relationships. He saw that they could initiate a helpful process in the client when representatives were directed or allowed to move spontaneously. With few questions it was possible to reintegrate excluded family members and promt short dialogues of resolution.

Constellations

The basic procedures for doing a constellation are actually very simple. In the context of a therapy or personal development group, clients are asked to choose representatives for those people who are important to their issue, including a representative for themselves, and to place them in a spatial relationship to one another. These may be members of the person's family of origin, which could include the client, siblings and parents, or perhaps only the person's parents and the client. Sometimes a constellation represents only the client and some symptom of distress. The client chooses the representatives from the people present in the group and, without any comment, positions them within the working space. The person should do this according to a feeling, or some inner sense of what is right, without regard to any reasons for this placement and without consideration of any particular time or any images of historical "scenes" from their family life. The person simply keeps an open heart and follows whatever inner impulse might arise. Normally, it needs to be clear who is representing which person or abstraction (abstractions might include a symptom such as anxiety, or an abstract concept such as "the secret" or "death").

The therapist may ask the client for information about the family history before the beginning of the constellation in order to get a feeling for the "weight" of the elements and to determine which family members should be included in the constellation from the start. The less the representatives know about the facts, the more convincing their feeling responses, but a constellation usually receives the initial impulse from some essential information. Surprisingly, experience has shown that the course of the constellation is more influenced by the feelings and sensory awareness of the representatives than by the information provided by the client or the therapist's initial conjectures.

When the representatives have been positioned, the client sits down again and watches from outside the working area. After a brief pause to allow everyone to collect themselves, the therapist asks the representatives to report what they are feeling, or any physical symptoms they might be aware of. They may be asked to respond verbally or with a physical expression of some impulse or movement, or with some combination of the two.

In this process, the wisdom of the client's soul and the "soul" of the family can be seen, felt and experienced through its effects and influence. This experience is available to the client, the therapist, and everyone in the group. The key factor is whether the movements of the representatives, independent or prompted by the therapist, reveal the dynamics operating in the family's soul and eventually ease the difficulties and lead to an image of resolution. If this process of uncovering dynamics and moving towards resolution begins to stagnate, the therapist has to intervene. Additional representatives for other family members might be included, referring back to the information provided earlier by the client. For example, the therapist might decide to include the client's grandparents, or a one-time fiancée of the client's father, or might ask the client for additional information and change the composition of the constellation accordingly. New characters may be added, such as a deceased aunt who had once been in a psychiatric hospital.

The constellation comes to rest when the members of the client's family have moved from their fateful dynamics to find their way to each other with love and respect, when excluded family members have been re-integrated, and when each member of the family has found an appropriate place.

When the dynamics and the path to resolution are clear, the client is often put into the constellation in place of his or her representative, to experience the ease of standing in a good place in a reconciled or newly organised system. In addition to the movements of the representative that point towards the future, resolutions often demand some kind of ritual. This may include bowing down in respect and acknowledgement or brief communications between particular family members, or between the client and others in the family, especially his or her parents. Such rituals allow the soul to move in the direction of a good resolution, but the spoken words also make very clear to the client what it is that binds him or her to the system and what can bring about resolution.

A Case Example

A young man came into a group hoping to improve his relationships with women, and to find more joy in living. As the man answered questions about his relationship to women, his professional situation, and about his family of origin, the therapist commented that what stood out was how much effort the client put into his life. The man nodded. The therapist asked him to choose representatives for his family and place them in relationship to each other.

The man put his own representative to the right of his mother, his father at some distance on the other side, and his younger sister in front of his father, facing the same direction.

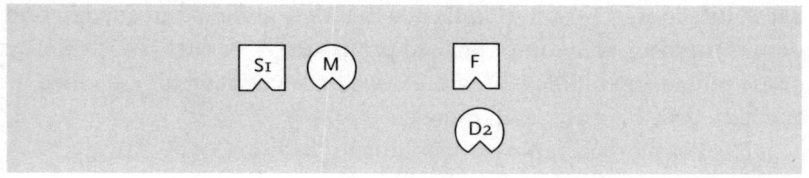

F = father   S1 = elder son (client)
M = mother   D2 = younger daughter

Diagram 1

After a brief pause, the representatives reported the following:

Father: My daughter has all my attention. I am not aware of anything
and I have no feelings at all towards my wife. I feel cut off and I
would be happiest if I left.

Mother: Having my son next to me feels good. He's warming me up. I
don't feel anything towards my husband or my daughter. It would
be fine with me if it were just my son and myself.

Son: I don't feel well. I feel almost sick, and I'm angry. I would like to
scream. I can't stand it here; I have to leave. (He moves spontaneously two steps to the right, away from the mother.)

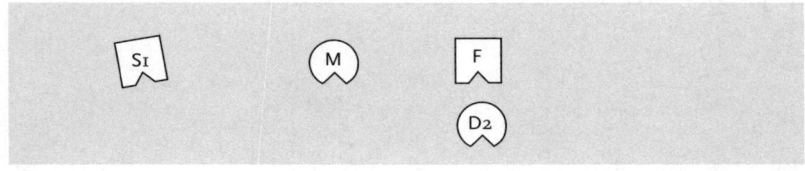

F = father   S1 = elder son (client)
M = mother   D2 = younger daughter

Diagram 2

Daughter: It feels nice and warm having my father behind me. I'd like
to lean back and close my eyes, and have him take me in his arms.
(She does this and the father's representative holds her.)

The therapist points out to the client, who is sitting next to him in the
group, that all the representatives in the constellation are looking in the

same direction. This often indicates that they are looking at someone who is missing, someone who died prematurely, or who was struck by some other difficult blow of fate. He asks the client what happened in his family, or his parents' families.

The young man reports the following facts about his family:

His maternal grandfather left his wife (the client's mother's mother) when his mother was seven years old. His mother saw her father a few more times, but then he re-married and the contact was lost. When the client's mother was 16, her father died. Neither his mother nor his grandmother attended his grandfather's funeral because they did not learn of his death until some time later.

The client's paternal grandmother died when his father, an only child, was five years old. The grandfather took care of the child for a while, but then he had to give the boy to his dead wife's sister. This aunt had no children of her own and she and her husband adopted the child (the client's father). They lost contact with the boy's natural father and his fate is unknown.

On the basis of this information, the therapist makes some changes in the constellation. He adds a representative for the mother's father and puts him in the place where the son had originally been standing. Then he moves the daughter somewhat off to the side and in her place he puts a representative for the father's mother.

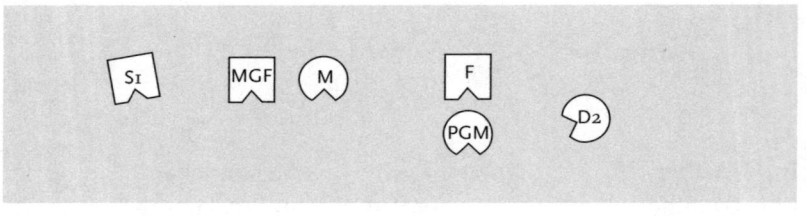

F	=	father	PGM	=	paternal grandmother
M	=	mother			(father's mother)
S1	=	elder son (client)	MGF	=	maternal grandfather
D2	=	younger daughter			(mother's father)

Diagram 3

The client's mother spontaneously turns towards her father and snuggles up to him like a little girl. She sighs deeply and then smiles happily.

The father's mother, however, moves forward as though sleepwalking until she bumps into someone sitting in the group. The daughter looks at her grandmother and begins to take a step forward, but then remains in her place, albeit uneasily. The client's father shuts his eyes and becomes very rigid. The therapist, without speaking, takes the father and leads him to follow his mother (the client's grandmother). After a while, the father reaches out to his mother from behind her and, still with his eyes closed, leans his head on her back. The therapist has the grandmother turn around. She looks at her son and takes him in her arms. The father begins to weep and after struggling with himself about whether to defend himself or to give in, he finally presses himself close to his mother and slowly becomes calm. The daughter has tears in her eyes and she follows her father. She lays her hand comfortingly on his back as if she were his parent.

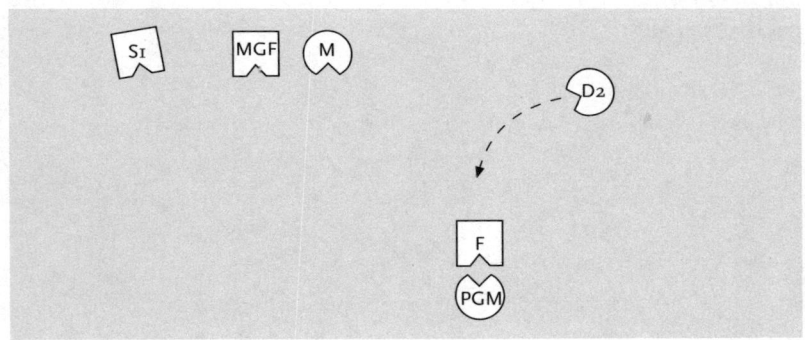

F	=	father
M	=	mother
S₁	=	elder son (client)
D₂	=	younger daughter

PGM	=	paternal grandmother (father's mother)
MGF	=	maternal grandfather (mother's father)

Diagram 4

The son seems rather uninvolved and when asked says:

Son: It's good for me to have my mother's father. I'm relieved that he's there and I feel better. All that with my father is somehow rather far away from me.

The mother now stands up straight next to her father and says:

Mother: Now, for the first time, I have some feeling for my husband and I notice that he is missing from my side. I'd like it if he would come back. It feels very good and very secure with my father here next to me.

The therapist leads the father back to a position next to his wife and places his mother very near behind him, but in a place where she can see her grandchildren. He places the two children in front of their parents. The son is standing opposite his father and the daughter opposite the mother. He moves the mother's father a bit off to the side and adds a representative for the mother's mother to stand behind the mother. He arranges the representatives in order, so that the mother's father, who died young, can be seen, but has a place somewhat apart from his daughter and his first wife. The mother's mother strengthens her daughter and the father's mother stands behind her son, giving good support.

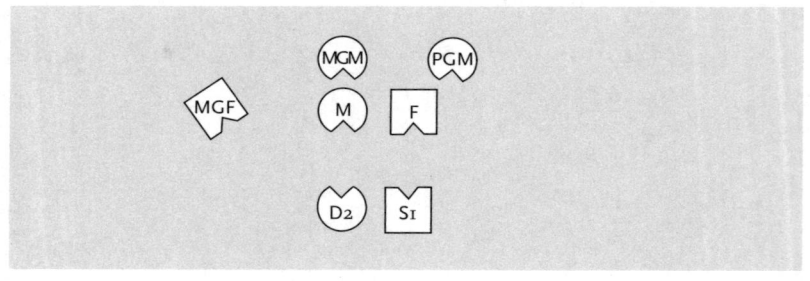

F	=	father		PGM	=	paternal grandmother
M	=	mother				(father's mother)
S1	=	elder son (client)		MGF	=	maternal grandfather
D2	=	younger daughter				(mother's father)
				MGM	=	maternal grandmother
						(mother's mother)

Diagram 5

The therapist asks the representatives for their feedback:

Father: The warmth that I felt earlier from the front, from my daughter, is now coming from behind, from my mother, and that feels very good. I am aware of my wife now and for the first time I can really see my children, especially my son. Somehow, I feel a bit proud now. Still, my legs are rather weak.

Mother: I feel good having my mother at my back, but my husband is too far away from me. I'm not happy with this. In some way we are a family now, but I feel an unsatisfied longing and my son is too far away. There is still something between my husband and me, as if there's something keeping us apart.

Son: I feel much better here now that I've got a father, and my grandmother's look of love touches my heart. When my mother looks so longingly at me, I feel weak. Generally speaking, I could use some strength. Perhaps another man near my father...? My grandfather? (The therapist adds a representative for the father's father and places him at the father's side, but at a distance.)

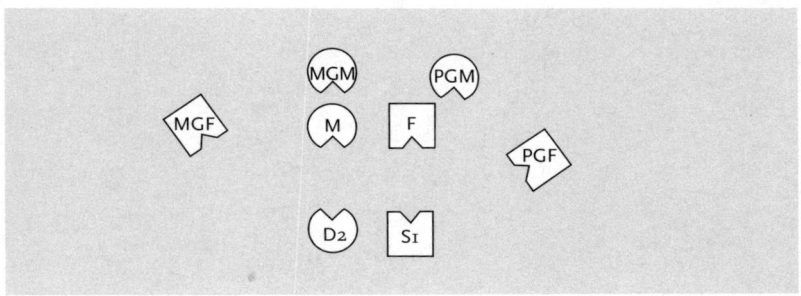

F	=	father
M	=	mother
S1	=	elder son (client)
D2	=	younger daughter
PGM	=	paternal grandmother (father's mother)

MGF	=	maternal grandfather (mother's father)
MGM	=	maternal grandmother (mother's mother)
PGF	=	paternal grandfather (father's father)

Diagram 6

Son: Yes, that's very, very good. (He beams at his grandfather, who smiles back at him.) Now there's a good balance there.

Daughter: I feel much better. The two grandmothers are good to have. Now my daddy is being taken care of and I don't have to worry about him. Now I can actually live. My mummy is still missing something.

The therapist asks the client if either of his parents had had a relationship with someone else before they got married, or if anything else occurs to him that could be pertinent. The client says that his father did not have a relationship before he married his wife. He was somewhat younger that the client's mother. The man vaguely remembers his mother having once spoken about a fiancé who had left her. Otherwise, nothing occurs to him. But, in case it should happen to be important, his mother had an abortion after his sister was born. His mother had told him about that recently, after a row with his father. He had the impression that she felt guilty about the abortion. The therapist chooses a representative for the mother's one-time fiancé and places him next to the client's mother.

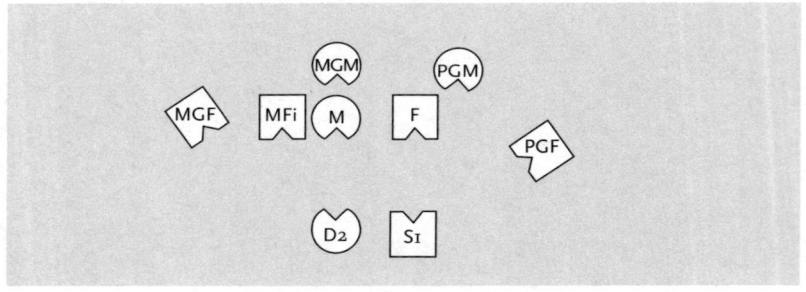

F	=	father	MGF	=	maternal grandfather
M	=	mother			(mother's father)
S1	=	elder son (client)	MGM	=	maternal grandmother
D2	=	younger daughter			(mother's mother)
PGM	=	paternal grandmother	PGF	=	paternal grandfather
		(father's mother)			(father's father)
			MFi	=	mother's fiancé

Diagram 7

The mother lays her head on this man's chest in the same way she had put her head on her father's chest. She becomes very teary. The therapist asks her to look at the man and say to him: "I miss you. I loved you very much. Despite the pain of your leaving, I have always longed for you. Now it's time for me to truly let you go. I will remember you fondly." The therapist leads the ex-fiancé off to the side, but still turned towards the others and clearly seen by them all. He moves the father a bit nearer the mother.

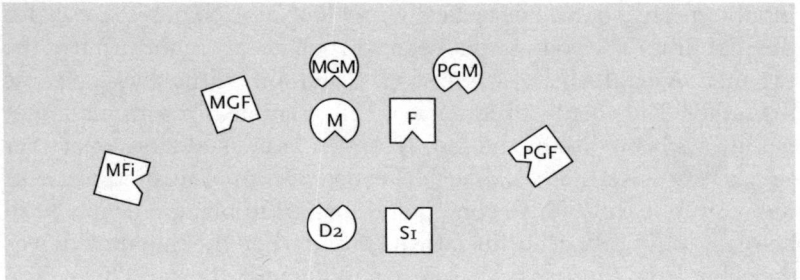

F   = father
M   = mother
S1   = elder son (client)
D2   = younger daughter
PGM = paternal grandmother
       (father's mother)

MGF = maternal grandfather
       (mother's father)
MGM = maternal grandmother
       (mother's mother)
PGF = paternal grandfather
       (father's father)
Mfi = mother's fiancé

Diagram 8

The therapist then asks the mother to look at her son and say to him: "My dear son, you have been my comfort. Whenever I look at you I feel a bit of my love and longing for my father and my ex-fiancé. Your presence has always been a relief for me, but now I release you. With my father in my heart and my mother close by, I am fine. I am letting go of my old fiancé along with the old pain and the old longings. I leave you to your dad."

The client, who is sitting in the group, exhales visibly.

Finally, the therapist adds a representative for the aborted child and places this person on the floor in front of the two parents, leaning back against them. Both the father and the mother spontaneously lay their hands on the child's head. They look directly and warmly at each other for the first time.

The client is asked to assume the place of his representative in the constellation. He stands quietly for a while and puts his arm around his sister. He then leaves her and goes to his father's father, takes him by the hand and leads him to the grandfather's son (the client's father). Silently he embraces the two. The therapist firmly removes the client's arms from the embrace and moves him back. He asks the father and grandfather to embrace the client instead of him embracing them. They do so energetically, and look at each other openly for the first time. The young man begins to sob deeply in the arms of the two men. A great tension seems to relax and something thaws towards his father. The client's experience of his relationship with his father has always been distant and indifferent and now, suddenly, his father seems very close and he can feel love towards him. The therapist asks the man to leave off his sobbing and instead to breathe deeply until he really, physically feels his father. After a while the therapist moves the client from the arms of his father and grandfather, and turns him around in front of them so he can feel them at his back. The young man straightens up visibly, his face lightens up, and he nods firmly to the therapist.

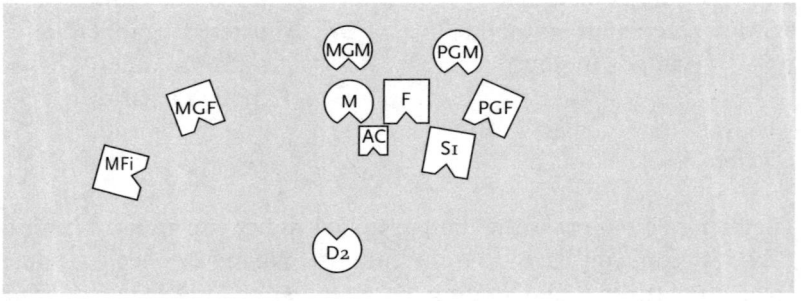

F	=	father	MGM =	maternal grandmother (mother's mother)
M	=	mother		
S1	=	elder son (client)	PGF =	paternal grandfather (father's father)
D2	=	younger daughter		
PGM	=	paternal grandmother (father's mother)	Mfi =	mother's fiancé
			AC =	aborted child
MGF	=	maternal grandfather (mother's father)		

Diagram 9

The constellation ends here.

In this 30-minute constellation, the client and the rest of the group could clearly see a great deal about the dynamics in this family. Many of the group participants nodded knowingly, and some had tears in their eyes. There was no need for the therapist to explain anything.

The information provided, the movements, and the spoken communication in the constellation brought sufficient clarity about what the bonds had been in this family and what would leave this young man freer and stronger. His original issue was that his relationships with women had been very unsatisfactory; he had had many girlfriends, but he always felt pulled back from them and the women always felt angry with him for being so unreachable and for refusing to hold up his side of the relationship. He was very successful in his professional life, but that did not bring him joy and a sense of security. Now, he could at least guess at the connections and, more importantly, he could take his rightful place. From this place, having looked at the fate that belonged to his family, he could feel his loving connection to his parents and experience a new vitality and trust in life.

Analysis

We can, of course, analyse this constellation with hindsight. What had happened in this family?

The client's mother had lost her father at a very early age when her parents separated. At first there was minimal contact with him, but after a while there was none, and then he died. She continued to feel a childlike love and longing for him. Some of these feelings were re-activated in her relationship to her fiancé, but there was a repetition of the earlier childhood situation when he left her. Still, she continued to keep her love and longing for him in her heart, just as for her father. Then, her son came along and took the place of her father and ex-fiancé, and she continued to love them in her son. For the client, that provided a tremendous closeness to his mother, but he felt this as a burden as well. In addition, he experienced his father as lacking in strength and too occupied with himself to free his son from his excessive closeness to his mother.

The client's father was left in a kind of blind numbness and absence of feelings after the death of his mother, which is a reaction we often see in people who have lost their mothers when they were children. He was well taken care of later by his adoptive parents but, over time, the adoption led to a complete separation from his father in addition to the loss of his mother. He felt abandoned and alone, and closed off his feelings. If he let his love flow, he re-experienced his pain and longing for his mother again and felt drawn to follow her into death. This was his deep, justifiable fear.

The daughter in the family felt the pull towards death behind her father's hidden feelings. She put all her energy into fighting against this pull and tried to keep her father alive by staying close to him and giving him what he had been denied with his mother. In doing so, she sacrificed part of her carefree childhood and her closeness to her own mother. In her late teens she had to be treated for depression and had a brief bout of anorexia, but recovered. At the time of this constellation, she had been married for two years and was very often ill.

The bonds of the two children with the fates of their parents also separated the sister and brother. Each one had a "task" but they had lost the feeling of simply being the two children of their parents. The actual relationship between the siblings was not problematic, but rather distant. The resolution that emerged in the constellation for the parents was a great relief for the children. They could now, retroactively, hold a mental image of their place as children. The grandparents were granted a place, and the family's love could flow freely through the proper channels, according to the various fates of those concerned.

This explanation of the family dynamics is, of course, not a complete picture of the family's reality. The family members seem to have unmet needs, even in the experience of the constellation itself. It is clearly not necessary to elucidate the dynamics of a constellation for a client with any explanations of this kind. Explanations have much more vitality when they are experienced indirectly through the movements of the representatives and the words that are spoken. In the evolving course of the constellation, one can feel immediately what is right and what isn't, and the therapist can correct any prior assumptions according to the reactions of the representatives and the client. One need not delve into any aspects of the family dynamics except those that clearly provide relief. The greatest advantage of the constellation method is the focus on what is essential and experiential. Actual experience and the accompanying insight replace that kind of thinking and reflection that goes no further than the head.

When we look at a constellation like this one, we can imagine that the logical conclusion will be changes in the client's relationship to women, his professional life, and of course his relationship to his parents, who are still alive and living together. Other questions may arise, however. In groups, participants often ask if the effects are really helpful to someone, beyond the experience of the constellation and, do representatives reliably reflect what happened in the client's family? If that is so, how is it possible? What happens if there is no relevant information about a family's history? Are those events in the family history really more influential than what we experience directly in growing up with our parents? I will return to these and other questions later.

From Classical Constellations to "Movements of the Soul"

The constellation described above is an example of what we would call a "classical" family constellation. In the development of constellation work, new aspects have emerged that essentially refine a constellation more to an event horizon, the furthest point from which effects can be felt in relationship to the fundamental presenting issue or the client's life situation. The constellation is then left more to the free movements of the representatives, even in terms of finding new orders and resolutions. Sometimes very little information, perhaps just a single fact, is gathered before, during, or after a constellation. Some constellations proceed silently, in confidence that the physical images of whatever happens with the representatives will be clear enough to the client. Any interpretations or interventions by the therapist are radically reduced.

To illustrate this kind of work, I will describe a constellation that, although very brief and simple, is one of the most moving constellations I have ever led.

A man, a psychotherapist himself, had been experiencing a powerful death wish ever since his 21-year-old sister's suicide and the subsequent sudden illness and death of his father. The man was asked to set up representatives for his mother, his father, his sister, and himself. No other information was requested.

The man placed his father and sister close to one another, his representative at a distance, looking at the other two, and his mother close behind him. After a short while, his sister looked at her father with unbelievable warmth and love. She pressed up close to him, kissed him, and then lay down in front of him with her eyes closed. The father looked at daughter lying before him and began to weep, quietly, but so deeply that there was scarcely a person in the entire group without tears in their eyes.

The man stood there crying for about five minutes, and then lay down next to his daughter on the floor. The two embraced warmly. The client's representative moved over to the two and lay on the floor on the other side of his sister. Although she barely noticed him, he lay there completely relaxed. After a while, I then asked him to stand up and go over next to his mother. He stood in that place, and then nodded his head. After another brief period of complete silence, I ended the constellation.

What happened here? Why was everyone so deeply touched? There were no questions from the client or the group. The client seemed very relaxed. He too had wept, while watching attentively from outside the constellation. The expression of sorrow, so closed and burdened, that had been on his face before the constellation had wholly disappeared by the end. He seemed to understand completely, even though he did not know what had really happened in his family, or what had so drawn his father and his sister together in death. According to feedback at a later date, his death wish had dissolved and he experienced a new surge of vitality.

What happens in a constellation?

- It begins with an issue, or a need, or the client's desperate search for resolution. The "weight" of the issue is what carries the entire constellation. The way the client formulates the issue and the accompanying gestures provide the first important information for the therapist, and the therapist's first accurate feedback in response to the "energy" of the client usually creates a basis of trust for the process to follow.
- A few brief questions establish the "field" of the constellation, that is, the persons that will be represented, and the dynamics of the psychic relationships that seem to be involved.
- As many representatives are placed in the field as seems necessary for a starting point, at least one person, but more usually two or more. There may also be representatives of symptoms, feelings, secrets, death, war, countries, or other abstractions.
- When positioned, the representatives open themselves up to the forces operating within the field and express, physically or with words, whatever they are aware of. There may be a fluid exchange between free movements and spontaneous statements, and expressions guided by the therapist.
- These movements may lead naturally to a resolving step that is ripe for expression, for example, an embrace for a mother or daughter following a long-standing animosity. Or, the therapist

might follow an inner image or some feeling about what is called for, and may guide a representative in a particular movement or to a new position to check out the reactions of the representatives and the client.

- The therapist may intervene by asking the client additional questions, which could prompt changes in the representatives' positions or the addition of new representatives. He or she may initiate a ritual, such as bowing down, or provide sentences that make the bonds within the system clear, or sentences of resolution. The therapist may arrange the constellation into an image of resolution in order to provide a new orientation and a place for everyone in this relationship system.

- Occasionally, a constellation needs to be broken off because the representatives have become very confused or cannot feel their way into the system, or because all movement stagnates and no new information is forthcoming. Sometimes, we stop because a client is unable to feel anything or make any connection with the constellation.

- When it seems necessary for clarity and understanding for the client and the group, the representatives may be asked for additional comments after the constellation, or the therapist might comment upon some aspect of what has happened.

- The therapist can check out his or her sense of what is going on by asking the client directly for a reaction. If it is useful, there can be a follow-up intervention, such as a guided fantasy that picks up on cues from the constellation and provides the resolving step. "Close your eyes and imagine your mother. Look at her and tell her..." or, "imagine your father..."

- If a constellation does not give the client something new, as a rule we cannot expect it to have any effect.

- Generally, this is the end of the "help" for the client, but there are many exceptions. There may be individual follow-up sessions, additional group constellations, letters, or telephone consultations. The actual process of resolution is reflected in the client's behaviour following the constellation and in real changes that occur in the person's state and in relationship systems.

In Chapter 4, I will provide a more detailed description of this method of working, but for anyone learning the approach and trying to understand the many facets of the process, it would, of course, be useful to experience many constellations, perhaps in an advanced training programme. The literature list at the end of this book offers additional resources.

Here, I only mean to make clear that constellations with representatives proceed simply and intensively on their own, without any instructions to the representatives (for instance, we do not tell them to hold hands, or kneel down, or stand on a chair). Such movements may occur in a constellation but only when they evolve from the representatives' feelings. Then, the movements carry weight and conviction because they reflect something that belongs to the relationship system or the client. It should also be clear here that a constellation constructs itself from the factual events and fates in a family, with the help of minimal interventions by a therapist.

What is most important is that constellations can show us, in a new, convincing form, how the fate of others in our relationship network affects us and creates problems, and how forces for change can be awakened through insight into previously unconscious processes. The therapist cannot plan any of this in advance. The therapist, the representatives, and the client all enter into a process without preconceptions, intentions, expectations, fear, or well-intended protectiveness. It is a process whose outcome cannot be seen in advance but one that is aimed towards an unknown resolution. Whether representatives are free to move spontaneously or whether the therapist intervenes with an image or hypothesis, the focus always remains on the effects, which then dictate the next step. Whether it is more appropriate to allow the representatives to move freely or for the therapist to guide them, depends on the observable, felt effects on the client. These effects, however, do not remain static, but immediately become part of a multi-layered process, the interplay between setting one's life course and having it set by events and dynamics beyond one's control. When a constellation helps, the effects set a course towards changes that can bring resolution.

3 Bonding and Resolution

Constellations basically look at two questions. Firstly, what entangles one family member in the fate of another and what might resolve this entanglement? Secondly, what is needed to support a free flow of love? These basic questions unfold in a multitude of different ways in constellation work.

In relationships and, therefore, in our souls, we are deeply bound to others. This is especially true in families and other relationships where there is an existentially significant exchange of giving and taking. Events of earlier times and places continue to be present and work in our souls, unconsciously as well as consciously, and influence our experience, feelings, thoughts and actions. We are well aware of this phenomenon and, at least in recorded history, our understanding of it has been part of the human experience.

What binds us to one another? What happens when we try to dissolve such bonds, and is that even possible? How do bonds influence us, and in what ways are they helpful or harmful? Can we free ourselves from bonds at all, even if they are harmful? If this is possible, how do we do it? What binds us to the dead, and what releases us from them? What ties us to old pain, guilt, and trauma (not only what we have experienced ourselves, but also what has been experienced by those we love, and to whom we are bound in some way)? How can we free ourselves of this old suffering, or from a compulsive repetition of the disturbance that intrudes into new life situations and interferes with our response to new events?

Family constellations go beyond the concept of a purely personal experience of trauma to include trauma that has been the fate of others, primarily those we are bound to in empathy and blind love and in a kind of unconscious attempt to balance and compensate. This, too, extends beyond the limits of present time and space. Love and its consequences is the theme that runs through being a man or a woman, relationships between parents and children, the flow of life and love through generations, and the obstacles that stand in its way. Constellations help us look at life and death, at our tragedies, at justice, guilt and atonement, at victims and perpetrators, good and evil, truth and lies, secrets and ruthless exposure, hate and reconciliation, and at positive and negative compensations. We are concerned with what it means to be alone or bound in relationship, with looking back and looking forward, with satisfaction and happiness, and with anxieties, depression and despair. We look at everything that is significant in our soul in terms of the important events in our lives. We focus on those things that are a danger to us and prevent us from living more fulfilled lives. We look forward towards what might free us to some degree from our problems. Constellation work is focussed on what fate and pure chance have dealt us, and what has developed out of our own choices, with whatever degree of freedom we may have had.

What has already been determined for us in our lives? When something in the past stands between us and our future, how can we allow it to recede into the background so that our view forward is not distorted by that past, but carried by it? What "regularities" do we find operating in fate, and what "order" helps love to flow? How do we find equilibrium between those forces in our mind and soul that bind us, and those that free us?

All these questions appear in family constellations, embedded in the systemic connections. The answers are not sought at the personal, autonomous level of one individual, but in the interconnected relationships of family and society, and the events that influence them. The focus, of course, is always on love. Love is the fundamental characteristic of human life and soul, expressed in the continuation of life, growth, biological conditions, the laws of physics, systemic organisation, and in everything that allows us to survive, physically and mentally, and to pass on our genes.

I will describe some of the experiences that have occurred in constellations to illustrate the "laws" of bonding and resolution in relationships and, therefore, in our soul, but before I move on to that, I want to say a few words about the term "soul".

The Soul

There has been conspicuously little said about the soul in the traditional fields of psychology and psychotherapy. Although the functioning of the brain, and to a certain extent behaviour and feelings, are operable concepts, the term "soul" is not. Additionally, many associate the word soul with some immortal core and since "God is dead" the soul must be dead as well. I find it, therefore, rather surprising how often this word is used in the media and in what context. Here we find that what is meant is not individual feelings or a personal, immortal "core", but rather a process of group identity. We read about the "damaged soul of Cambodia", or the "soul of Europe" or the "soul" of a football match.

We experience the soul (whether we use that word or not) similarly in family constellations, from a systemic perspective. We could call soul the invisible force that includes the whole in each part, and that which makes the whole more than the sum of its parts and functions. It is not identical to consciousness because it includes the unconscious. It is not the same as the physiological and physical processes in our bodies and brains, although it is inseparably connected to them. It is not the same as our feelings, although feelings are an experiential expression of the soul. It is not the "core" or the "essence" of the whole, but rather what contains the whole, an all-encompassing space. It is the "field" of everything that affects a person or a group over space and time that connects and creates identity.

One could speak of an individual soul as that which makes the person that particular person, including everything that belongs to him or her: body, brain, mind, thoughts, feelings, actions, experiences, and history – everything that comprises the word "I".

We can also speak about a family soul, and it is this soul that is the realm of family constellations. This includes everything that makes a family a particular family over space and time. It includes all the family members, the events and experiences, memories, decisions, and so on.

In a similar way we could talk about the soul of a clan, or an extended family, or the soul of a business, country, or culture. In every important aspect of our lives, from "I – you" to our relationship to nature or the universe, we are bound to various "soul" fields in a multitude of ways. The entire range of our connectedness is what Bert Hellinger often calls the "greater soul". What he is talking about in this regard is not some mystical, otherworldly power. It is the whole of individual, collective, and cosmic existence that animates and carries us, that binds, and perhaps even leads us. It is bigger than our understanding, and with increasing knowledge it begins to seem even more mysterious. In this concept of soul, there is a "knowing" that connects us, which goes beyond our conscious communication of information to include participation in the "knowing" of the whole, or a "knowing" part that is connected to the whole. Albrecht Mahr has referred to the "knowing field".

We cannot locate the soul using the methodology of natural science that looks for "nothing more than" in the search for parts and particles and their functional interactions. Our everyday experience is dependent on "more than". No conversation, art, politics, or relationship is independent of a soul experience. Because we cannot reduce soul experiences to concrete, quantifiable substances, we have developed "soul words" in our language, words like freedom, patience, spirit, courage, love, and so on. We cannot adequately capture what we mean by love by talking about genes or brain functions. We know that to communicate in a way that can be understood when we are dealing with the realm of the soul, we have to rely upon pictures, metaphors and imagery, personal experience and awareness, and subjective assessment. Although the natural sciences have led to new discoveries, and have forced us to more carefully examine mental processes such as the parameters of free will, our thinking about processes of the soul in actual human behaviour has remained more a concern of the humanities and a systematic analysis of life experiences. In the entire orchestra of psychological theory and practice, family constellation work is perhaps the approach most concerned with the soul and those mind-body forces that have an impact at this level.

Bonds of Love and Entanglements

We are bound to our groups in deep, mostly unconscious ways through conception, birth, and our inability to survive and grow without a group. The soul-force that holds a group together in order to produce, contain, and promote life is primarily a bond of personal love. It is an elemental force that serves group survival and the continuation and development of life, before we even have a chance to think about it or plan accordingly.

The energy and effects of this binding love are often markedly visible in family constellations in the process of entanglement. Entanglement is what brings someone, without knowledge or choice, to repeat or blindly enter into the fate of another person in the family or group system.

These bonds of love consider individuals only in terms of their function for the survival of the group, and they meet with two sources of conflict. First, there is a conflict with individual survival mechanisms, which is superseded by the group need to maintain and reproduce itself at the price of individual egotism. The second point of conflict is the empathy that group members feel towards each other as loving individuals, which holds them together. The conscious and unconscious binding forces function through conscience. In order to understand the theory and practice of constellation work, it is necessary to understand the fateful effects of these forces and bonds. Some of Bert Hellinger's most significant contributions include a new, contemporary view of the processes of bonding and entanglement as regulated by conscience, and the discovery of reconciling and integrating paths that can lead to resolution.

Conscience

Hellinger's concept of conscience is the most widely generalised of his insights from family constellation work. Conscience can be understood as an instrument of the soul for maintaining balance in relationships. We may be driven by our genetic code, which seems to have no function other than to protect itself and pass itself on, but we also remain connected by our relationships in a social field in which we have to act. Conscience is, generally speaking, the capability to evaluate behaviour according to the clan. It is etymologically a "collective knowledge", a "with-knowing" (from the Latin "conscientia" and Greek "syneidesis"). The term conscience emerged in ancient Greece in the assumption that an inner "knower" participated in all our dealings with other people and in relation to the gods. From this, Christian understanding developed an absolute God-given standard of good and evil.

Looking at human behaviour, however, it is clear that we may often do terrible things with a clear conscience, and a bad conscience may prevent us from doing good. Based on his experience with therapeutic processes, Bert Hellinger began to re-define the basic concept of conscience. Conscience only tells me what I have to do to secure my belonging to a group, and what I cannot do without risking punishment or exclusion from the group. Conscience can only measure the correctness of behaviour in terms of the needs and rules of belonging to one particular group. There are three discernible dynamics and three different levels of conscience, each with conscious and unconscious effects.

Three Dynamics of Conscience: Belonging, Balance, and Order
In terms of our *belonging* to a group, we have a good conscience when we do things that allow us to belong, to remain close to others and

under their care, and to be seen and respected as an equal. We have a bad conscience when we behave in a way that excludes us from the group, when we lose our security and closeness, or are threatened by some kind of probationary measures.

The dynamics of *balance and compensation* within the group include justice, the measure of giving and taking, and a sense of rights and responsibilities. We have a clear conscience when we have given something and therefore have a right to receive, or when we contribute to smoothing out imbalances and enabling a more just exchange. We have a bad conscience when we have taken and are now obligated to repay the debt, or when we have caused some imbalance or injustice that endangers the peace and cohesion of the group.

The concept of *order* in relationship systems looks at hierarchy or rank, and the reliability of our life together. We have a good conscience when we obey the rules and standards and act in a "conscientious" way. We have a bad conscience when we go against the hierarchy, orders, truths, taboos, and rules and risk punishment as a consequence.

The Three Levels of Conscience: Group conscience, Personal Conscience, and Universal Conscience

The different dynamics of conscience mentioned are all present in the three different levels of conscience: the personal conscience, the collective or group conscience, and the universal conscience. We do not know exactly how these three levels of conscience developed in the evolution of mankind, but we might suspect that conscience in the group first formed as a kind of instinctive steering mechanism for the group as a whole. It then perhaps grew to distinguish between individual people or groups, "I" and "you" or "we" and "they", and entered into conscious awareness. Finally, through the migrations, meetings and mingling of various peoples, it broadened to the scope of religious experience on earth and to the entire universe.

The group conscience pays no attention to any single person as an individual, but only to the group as a whole. Individuals are only important in terms of the function they perform for the group. This conscience works as a directional guide for an integrated, collective movement; imagine the movement of a flock of birds, or school of fish moving in harmony. The focus is the well-being and survival of the group and although each individual attends to the needs of the group, the group does not consider the needs of any individual. Today, we have very little awareness of this seemingly archaic conscience. It is as though it has sunk deep down into our inner being, or perhaps remains in the realm of biological field phenomena that work outside our conscious awareness to ensure survival and order. Many of the processes we see in constellations have to do with this family-clan-group conscience. Because we have no conscious awareness of the process, we can only recognise it by observing its effects on the group. As we become aware of it in this way, we also have the opportunity to consciously contribute to a positive movement towards resolution that remains in accordance with the group conscience, while leading beyond its narrow confines.

There have been several developments that have resulted in a shift of conscience from a general directional guide to an individual, "audible" authority. There has been increasing distinction within groups into various tasks, capabilities and internal relationships, an increasing emphasis on the importance of individual achievement and the development of what we call personality, and an unfolding of empathy and personal love. Our experience of this conscience is usually as a drive that informs our preferences. The importance of the individual has increased and relationships within groups have also become more important. The differing needs of individuals and sub-groups have to be coordinated with the demands of the whole group. A moral code is needed to bind individual members to the group, and to contain and regulate the increasingly complex network of relationships.

"Good" and "bad" are markers of proper behaviour within the group, but also the group's distinctiveness from other groups. "Good" is whatever serves the group and "bad" is anything that benefits another group that is competing for the same resources or space. The service that each individual renders that contributes to the group or sub-group is deemed good. Anything that violates the standards and so endangers the group, or any other member of the group, is defined as bad. Considering only the well being and morals of our own group allows us a clear conscience even when doing terrible things to other groups and their members, or to other members of our own group.

This conscience is ameliorated by empathy in human relationships, but often only within one's own group, or only between particular individuals within a sub-group. In comparison to the collective conscience, the personal conscience can be seen as "progress" because it allows for differentiation of individuals and includes personal love.

At the same time, it opens up great potential for conflict in personal relationships, group interests, and archaic fundamental orders.

A universal conscience, orientated towards oneness, is called for when differing groups come into contact with one another and form larger units such as countries. The increasing contact between these larger units makes it clear that we all share one earth, and we all come from one universal beginning. This conscience is concerned with individuals as human beings, in the sense of what is common to all human beings, but also with the greater whole that we all participate in. The value of the individual, a sense of belonging, empathy, and common knowledge extend throughout the world. Individuals cross borders and build bridges that extend beyond "I-you" relationships, family connections, group identification, or national, linguistic or cultural bonds. This conscience is directed towards participation in a common ethic. Perhaps this is what the apostle Paul meant by "the law engraved on their hearts". This human movement to recognise and identify with increasingly large groups is what Bert Hellinger means when he speaks of the movements of the soul, not just as a method that allows representatives to move freely, but as the movement that the representatives make towards resolution, beyond the limitations of individuals, couples or groups. We feel this movement as something light and non-emotional, with a certain feeling of overall "rightness". In the movements of the soul, directed by forces that encompass all of humanity, our experience of a group conscience or personal conscience is not absent, but transcended within this larger frame.

Each of the three different levels of conscience affects our lives in its own particular way. They work together and complement one another in their effects, orientation and flow, but they also conflict with each other. Even at the individual level of conscience there are opposing movements between, for example, what is demanded for belonging, and a different need to increase stability. In therapeutic work, it is often a question of which conscience, consciously or unconsciously, lies behind a problem. Which bonds, events and behaviour on the part of individual members and groups are producing these effects, and which dynamics of conscience, at which level, offers clues to a solution?

When parents have separated and children live with a mother who expresses her hurt by belittling her ex-husband, the children feel her hurt and have a good conscience when they avoid any contact with their father. The price, however, is a bad conscience in relation to their father. Siding with their father brings a clear conscience in that regard, but a bad conscience in relation to their mother. Personal conscience is of no use in a situation like this. What is needed is an awareness of the effects of the group conscience that looks at the bonds and the right to belong that connect all the members of the group, regardless of their opinion of each other.

Children whose actual parentage has been kept a secret have a right to know who their father is and to have contact with him. This right might clash with family taboos, or conflict with a mother's desire to protect the family. A fleeing family who have to leave a dead child unburied in order to save the rest of the family are in conflict with their personal love for this child, but also with the instinct to hold the group together, including the dead, and their desire to give this child a respectful place among the dead ancestors. A need to conform to the rules of a workplace, or a political situation, may violate the moral code of a family.

Resolving conflict usually requires an individual to step beyond the narrow confines of one conscience into a larger context or frame of reference. Sometimes, however, the solution lies in retracting from an overly large frame of reference in order to bring close relationships into order. Constellations have the potential to reveal multi-layered conflicts of conscience and bring them into awareness, so that solutions can be sought. Given freedom of movement and enough time, representative can tap into the deep knowledge shared by all human beings, to feel their way beyond the narrow bonds of the system in the constellation and reach a meta-solution. Or the therapist may call upon his or her awareness of the processes of bonding and resolution to make minimal interventions to guide representatives, and therefore the client, towards an appropriate solution.

The Effects of the Bonds of Fate

In his encounter with primal therapy, it became clear to Bert Hellinger that bonds in families were not established exclusively through children's direct experiences with their parents or caretakers. Using certain breathing techniques, we can reactivate powerful, usually childlike emotions, and an objective observer looking at that person's childhood might be at a loss to explain the strength of the current expression.

When we look back at the fates of other people in the person's family, however, the feelings often make perfect sense. We may also carry emotions within us that belong to someone else's experience rather than our own. If the fate of the other person (perhaps even someone we do not know) is brought to light and into awareness, we can learn to distinguish these feelings from our own experience. Feelings that have been taken over from another person do not respond to psychotherapeutic regression, and other psychotherapeutic methods have had little success in this area when they do not include this awareness of our connections to the fates of others.

The Circle of Those Who Are Bound by Love

Who belongs to the circle subject to the effects of bonding? We look for the answer by looking at the effects of exclusion in the relationship system. If an excluded person has effects on the fate of others, it indicates that the person belongs to the system. Based on the experiences of family constellations, there seems to be a circle of people who could be defined as family, and belonging to a family. These include: the children, including any half siblings; the parents and their siblings and half siblings; the grandparents and sometimes their siblings as well; often also the great-grandparents; and now and again, even earlier family members.

The family circle, as a collective soul, is not restricted to direct bloodlines, living or dead. It also includes everyone who belongs on the basis of loss or gain, or who is existentially connected. This might include previous partners of parents or grandparents insofar as they have opened up a place for later partners. Adoptive parents may also belong and, under certain circumstances someone else, such as a war comrade who had to be left behind and died, although the father in this family escaped and survived. A young person who, for example, causes a traffic accident in which another person dies, then often belongs to that person's family system in this sense of fateful bonds. This is significant in terms of the fates of perpetrators and victims and the effects on later, sometimes distant generations.

In determining who belongs to the circle of those bound by love, we ask who is to be thanked for life and survival, and who has been responsible for serious injury or death? Who has been granted life and survival, and who was subjected to existential trauma or death?

Excluded Persons and Their Representatives

When a person in a family system has been excluded or denied an equal right to belong, or when someone's fate has been kept a secret (perhaps a suicide), the group conscience co-opts someone else, usually someone born later, to represent the excluded family member. This person is involved without conscious awareness and certainly has not consciously chosen to take on this task.

But why is it necessary for someone born later to represent an earlier excluded person in a way that causes him or her to feel like the other and in some way to share that person's fate? It is as though the function is to maintain an awareness, empathy, and respect for the excluded member's fate, and to bring those aspects back into the community of the group. An equal right of all members of the group to belong, regardless of their fate, serves to preserve the unity of the group so necessary for survival.

This archaic-seeming group conscience gives those who are born earlier priority over those who come along later. Representation of excluded family members is aimed at restoring the wholeness of the group. It is a process that only makes sense at the level of soul, that is, extending beyond the limitations of time and space.

Such blind participation, dictated by the group conscience, can be fully repressed by the personal conscience in order to avoid feelings of pain or guilt. Constellations reveal the blind demands of the group soul in such a way that the personal conscience can allows the excluded and shunned to be acknowledged and given their place in the group and in the flow of love.

A common example is that children born to an unmarried woman are often excluded from their father's family group, and those same fathers are often excluded from whatever family the children grow up in.

> There was a woman suffering from cancer, who had always had the feeling she did not belong to her family and had no real place in life. In a constellation of her family of origin, the representative of her mother spontaneously said, "There is someone missing here by my husband." The therapist added a representative for another woman and had her stand next to the father in the constellation. Then the mother said, "There is still someone missing." Following a hunch, the therapist added a representative for a child. The mother then reported, "Now everyone is here". The client, however, knew nothing about any unknown siblings, so the therapist ended the constellation.

The woman felt unsettled about what had happened, so that evening she asked her father about it. He told her that when he was eighteen he had had an affair with a married woman who "initiated him into manhood". Shortly thereafter, he forgot all about that relationship when he was called into the army and went off to war. After the war, when he was already married to the client's mother, he got a letter from the other woman telling him that she had had a child as a result of their relationship and that she might bring the boy to meet him someday. She had not given him an address and he never heard from her again, so he just let the whole matter drop. In a later constellation, this boy was added to the family. Besides his pain, the representative also felt a warm-hearted connection to his siblings, which relieved the client greatly. I have no idea whether the client looked for or found this half-brother in reality. We also do not know what connection there might be between the exclusion of a family member and illness, but illness sometimes seems to function as atonement for one's own guilt or the guilt of someone else.

Another lovely young woman, told a group that her favourite fairy tale was "The Ugly Duckling" because that is how she had always felt as a child. This is a story about a baby who does not belong to the group, because it is actually someone else's baby. In this woman's constellation, her mother could not find any connection to her father, but felt a strong connection to another male representative that had been added by the therapist (again following a hunch). When the client was asked whether it was possible that her father was not her real father, she had no information to that effect, but said that she certainly resembled her father in appearance. The client felt relieved by the thought that some other man might be her father and she decided to ask her mother about it. She talked to her mother and discovered that she actually did have a different father. He was a man who had sublet a neighbouring flat for a period of time. After he moved out, he continued to visit the family frequently and had played with the client when she was a child. The client phoned later to report that she had sought out her natural father and got on very well with him.

During a seminar in Spain, a German psychologist described what had happened in her own family. Even as a young child, she had felt a strong need to go abroad. After leaving school, she enrolled as a psychology student at a university in Spain, and stayed on in the same city as a practicing psychologist. Recently, a Swedish woman about the same age as this woman had showed up at her father's door in Germany with the suspicion that he was her father. The Swedish woman had grown up in a very normal Swedish family, but at the age of 13 she told her mother that although she was fond of her father, she didn't feel like he was her father. Her mother admitted that it was possible that she had a different father and told the girl the name and address of an American man. When the Swedish girl was 19, she flew to America to look for this man, and confronted him and his family with the fact that she could be his daughter. The man remembered the relationship with the Swedish woman and, unlike the rest of his family, was very pleased about having a Swedish daughter. On the way back home, however, the young woman began to feel uneasy about the whole thing. Her mother then told her that, having thought more about it, there was another man that could possibly be her father. She gave her daughter the name of a German man with whom she had had a one-night stand when he was in Stockholm on business. After some years, the young Swedish woman got up her courage and travelled to Germany to find this man. A DNA test proved that he was actually her father.

The German psychologist laughed as she told the story and said that she and her siblings were delighted to have this new sister. Her mother had died long ago, so she never found out anything about it. Strangely enough, once this sister had turned up, the German woman felt for the first time that she might be able to live in Germany again.

Sometimes it is a mother who is excluded.

There was a young woman who was gathering the necessary official papers in order to get married, when she discovered that the woman who had brought her up was actually her birth mother's sister. Her real mother had died during her birth and her father had married his widow's sister. Although this was common knowledge in the family, no one had ever told the child what had happened or who her natural mother was. It is possible that they wanted to protect the child, as the constellation showed that the client was feeling a strong pull towards her dead mother. The truth had devastating effects initially. The woman cancelled her wedding invitation to her entire family, which led to further rows. The woman herself felt very unburdened by the events in the constellation that allowed her and her mother to come together in a loving way and then say goodbye. Afterwards, the young woman felt very moved and said that she hoped to get pregnant. She did in fact become pregnant and eventually re-established her relationship to her family.

It quite often happens that previous partners of parents are excluded. They belong to the system because they have opened up a space for the later partners to enter the family and if they are excluded, someone else may represent them.

There was a single woman who had had many problems in relationships. Men always left her because she had such an aggressive personality.

When asked about her family history, she reported that her father had abandoned his fiancée in order to marry her mother. The other woman never married and she remained angry with this man for the rest of her life.

There was a young man, suffering from a brain tumour, who came for an individual session on his wife's recommendation. The tumour itself was benign, but when removed, it always grew back again and the repeated surgeries presented a high risk factor for the young man. When he was asked what his issue was, he had no answer. Although he was a very pleasant young man, he seemed limp and lifeless. He spoke very quietly, almost in a whisper, and he appeared to have simply given up on his health problems. He was asked to set up a set of small figures in a constellation of his family of origin, including his mother, father, and himself as the only child. Even taking into account the use of inanimate figures, the constellation felt very "thin", and the therapist asked about any previous relationships of his parents. He quietly but emphatically stated that there was nothing. He said that his mother had once mentioned that she had had a friend before she met his father, but the man was a wimp and the client was sure that there had not been any real relationship between the two. Other than that, he was not aware of anything of note in the family history, and questions did not seem to stir any awareness or interest. Nothing seemed to elicit any energy that would indicate that there was something to work with. After a short, desultory conversation, the therapist ended the session. As the young man left the office, the therapist suggested that he might want to ask his parents if there had been anything significant before they married, since they were well over thirty when they married, and there did not seem to be any other promising avenue of enquiry.

Two weeks later the man phoned to say that he had talked to his parents and found out that his mother had been married previously and so had his father. The therapist asked if there were any children from those marriages, but the young man had not thought to ask about that. The therapist suggested that since he had gone this far, he might as well ask about that as well. Again, two weeks passed before the young man phoned again, but this time something was quite different and his voice was strong and firm. He said that he had discovered that he had a brother from his father's prior marriage and, without consulting his father, he had found this man and called him. His brother was not very enthusiastic about it, but had agreed to meet with the client and they had made arrangements for a meeting.

We cannot possibly know whether the unknown relationships of his parents or this unknown brother had any causal connection whatsoever to this young man's brain tumour. What was clear, however, was that there was a marked change in his voice, as if he had gained strength and energy through this discovery of a secret brother.

Siblings who have died prematurely are often forgotten, particularly miscarried babies or children who died at birth. It appears that a foetus becomes relevant to the system at about five months' gestation (this can actually be tested out in constellations). In some cases, they are never mentioned to the living children, or they are spoken of in a way that indicates that the children are not to ask about this topic. This may be due to the pain it causes, or from a feeling of shame or guilt, or a feeling that the dead child is not of particular importance. Siblings, especially children born directly after the deceased child, often have a vague feeling that something is missing and they find themselves unconsciously representing the missing child. This may take the form of a feeling of being unimportant, or of being in the wrong place, or sometimes even an inexplicable pull towards death. These children may feel close to a void, or may hold a life-long orientation towards the missing brother or sister. Later, in a man-woman relationship, the person often tries to fill this gap with a partner. Sometimes a child born later is given the same name as the deceased child, and the dead child is not counted as one of the children. In constellations it is very moving when we see that the representatives of these deceased children are not suffering from their death, but from not being seen and not having a place in their family. It is as if they can only find peace when they have been held in their parents' arms, acknowledged by their brothers and sisters, and recognised as having a rightful place with their particular fate.

A young homosexual man set up a constellation of his family of origin. Despite various changes in the constellation and the addition of representatives for two grandfathers who had died relatively young, the client's representative reported that something was still missing on his right-hand side, something very close. The client called his mother and discovered that before his birth as the "only" child in the family, a sister had been stillborn. The constellation was set up again with only the parents, the stillborn sister and the client. Weeping but radiant, the young man took his sister into his arms with such tenderness and warmth that the entire group felt moved. We might speculate that the young man had always unconsciously felt this deep inner connection and identification with his sister and this could have been connected in some way to his homosexuality. In any case, the therapist happened to meet the young man some time later and discovered that the man was now married to a woman. He laughingly remarked that this was "despite the therapeutic opinion that homosexuality is seldom amenable to change."

Another man had set up constellations of his present family and his family of origin on several different occasions, including once together with his wife, but he had never really arrived at any solution. His issue was that he had repeated affairs with other women even though he loved his wife and two children. One day, the man rang and asked if he could set up another constellation. His wife had left him in the meantime. At a family gathering, his mother had casually mentioned to him that he actually was a twin. He was so taken aback that he hadn't even asked her anything more about it. In the constellation, he set up his twin as a female according to his intuition that it might have been a sister. The positioning in the constellation was such that no one except his representative was looking at this child. The dead twin was also only able to look at her brother. They flew into each other's arms and held each other, weeping. After a long time the constellation was guided to an end in which this child also had a good place. The client felt very relieved by this. Some time later, he asked his mother again about this possible twin, but she said she couldn't remember anything.

Bert Hellinger once had a man in a group who very aggressively declared that he was going to kill his mother on that day. On another occasion, he avowed he was going to kill his father. The therapist asked him if anyone in his family had been killed. At first the man couldn't think of anything of that nature, but then vaguely remembered something about a child who may have been killed. The man called his elderly father and was told the story. When the client was one year old, his mother was in her sixth month of pregnancy. The doctor told his parents that there were complications and he could save either the mother or the baby boy, but not both. The parents decided to sacrifice the boy to ensure the mother's safety. When he had told the story, this man, a rather overweight architect, said, "I eat for two, and I have two complete families. I have two children with my wife and also two with another woman. Sometimes I live with one family, sometimes with the other. I built a semi-detached house for my first family, but the other half has stood empty ever since it was built. In my office I have had a second desk for another worker for a long time, but I have never had anyone use it. It is almost as if I have saved a place for my brother my whole life."

Another common occurrence is when a particular fate of a person is excluded from their families, even though the person's existence is acknowledged.

There was a man who was working as an aide in a psychiatric hospital, but felt very unhappy in this job. In preparation for doing a constellation, he began collecting information about his family and asked about an aunt whom nobody seemed to know anything about. Only then did he discover that she had been killed as part of the euthanasia programme in a psychiatric institute during the Third Reich. Through the constellation, it became clear to him what he was trying to make up for in the psychiatric hospital and who he was trying to take care of. Shortly thereafter, he changed to a non-psychiatric, medical hospital.

A man came in for counselling because his eighteen-year-old son had left home and was living with an old peddler. His son had always had problems in school, mostly because he acted very aggressively on behalf of those he regarded as having been unjustly treated. The father was now feeling concerned that the boy might kill himself. Being asked further, the father stated that his own father had lost a lot of property due to some kind of injustice, and after the war he was caught committing petty theft and locked up by the Americans for six months. During that time, his wife, who was pretty fed up with her life with this difficult man, met another very loving man. When the father was allowed to return home, he hanged himself in the attic several days later. The client, who was twelve at the time, was the one who had discovered his father's body.

The client had never told his own sons the story and insisted "... and they should never find out about it. I told them my father died of a heart attack". When the therapist pointed out to him that it might have some bearing on his son's attraction to suicide, the man was shocked. After a moment's thought, he said that his younger son had screamed at him at the dinner table, "When are you finally going to get out of here and make some room?" Suddenly the client could feel a possible connection between his parents' behaviour and his sons'. A few weeks later, he told his sons the truth about their grandfather. The elder son later registered for a group and did a constellation of his family, in which it was clear that there was a close bond between him and his grandfather.

A fate that is covered up or lied about puts pressure on a later family member to repeat this fate, or to do something that will bring it back into the family memory, as if it could be retroactively altered or reparations made. In such situations, remaining silent helps no one. In addition to consciously transmitted information, we also seem to have a much deeper awareness about the fates of others. Because this "inner knowing" conflicts with our conscious awareness, it leads to confusion, and we deal with the discrepancy by transferring the feelings to a completely different situation. These hidden, intuitive feelings can lead to a repetition of the secret fate, to feelings that are foreign to us, or sometimes to illness or behavioural symptoms.

A woman said that her eldest daughter, aged nine, had been adopted to replace a child who had died at birth. She told the therapist that the girl knew she was adopted. When asked about the child's natural mother, the woman said that when this child was born, her mother had sought out their family to give her child to them for adoption. Then the mother jumped off a high bridge to her death. When asked whether the child knew this, the woman said, "Of course not! You can't tell a child something like that!" The therapist's response was, "Why not? She knows it anyway." The woman was appalled, and recounted an incident that had happened a few weeks earlier. The family had been hiking in the mountains with another family. At the summit, the adopted daughter had gone round to a steep drop on the other side of the peak, which made her mother very uneasy. When the mother came round to the other side, the girl was standing with her eyes closed and her arms spread wide. She said, "Flying off down there must be wonderful."

Imitation

When there are problems that could have something to do with a systemic connection to someone else's fate, the therapist's first questions look for an earlier precedent in the family. "Who in the family felt similar to this at one time?" "Was there someone who lost everything?" "Was someone left alone?" As children we tend to become like our parents and other loved ones who are close to us. It is like an inner voice that says, "I want to be like you." This is not just a passive adaptation or an automatic learning process; it comes from the active efforts of the child to be close to family members, most of all, of course, to his or her parents. The child imagines that such closeness is only possible through imitating and sharing the parents' behaviour and their fate. A child also learns from his or her parents and wants to be allowed to be like them. This provides closeness and security, even if it is damaging to the child. This kind of closeness and this feeling of belonging, achieved by imitating someone of primary importance, are critically important for a child.

A mother complained of her daughter's scornful attitude, but after some consideration she laughingly admitted that she had been exactly the same when she was that age. In one case, a father was worrying about his son's poor school performance and his secretive behaviour, but then remembered that he had been the same way as a child. He said, "Yes, it's true, I did the same thing." This man's mother had died when he was three years old and, between the ages of five and eight, he had secretly dressed up in his stepmother's clothes. This, of course, was a sign of his deep connection to his forgotten mother.

Children are often relieved to discover that their parent experienced similar difficulties as a child, particularly if they see that things have turned out well for their mother or father.

Following Another

There is a movement that is frequently seen in constellations when a representative is led out of the system, a few steps away, as a symbol of their death, or when someone is asked to lie down on the floor, as a symbol of their death. (Often, this movement takes place without any intervention from the therapist.) Frequently, another representative follows that person, moving to stand behind or next to the dead person, or lying down next to them on the floor. This is sometimes done without the slightest sign of emotion, but sometimes in tears, or beaming with joy. It is a sign of our willingness to follow another into death, and it most often involves children who are following their parents, particularly a parent who has died prematurely. We recognise this phenomenon in older couples, where it seems more understandable that when one of the two dies, the other also wants to die, longing to join the deceased partner. Many people experience such feelings, to a greater or lesser degree of consciousness, when a loved one or someone close dies earlier than seems right.

When a mother or father dies prematurely (sometimes other close relatives), it is as if something in the child's soul says, "Dear Mummy (or Dear Daddy), I want to be with you." The child knows intuitively that the parent can never come back to life, but dying oneself is still an option. If the child cannot let go of the closeness to the deceased person, an inner voice says, "Dear Mummy/Daddy, I will follow you and I won't be alone and you won't be alone. I will die, too." Sometimes a child actually dies, or becomes seriously ill, or perhaps speaks openly about a longing for death. Such a child may actually commit suicide at a later date, or might finally find release as an adult by dying early of a fatal disease or in an accident. If the child lives to normal old age, there may be a life-long sense of longing for death. Anyone close to such an individual feels this yearning for death and will probably become fearful.

A middle-aged woman set up a constellation of her family of origin. It became clear in the constellation that the woman felt drawn to join her deceased father, who had died of a sudden illness shortly after her third birthday. In the constellation, there was a loving and resolving encounter with her dying father and afterwards the woman seemed quite relaxed and cheerful. She then told the group an anecdote: "A few months ago I had a serious car accident. A car came speeding up behind me on the motorway and rammed into the back of my car. Thank God, no one was seriously hurt in the accident. As my car was skidding out of control, however, only one word came up from deep inside me. Finally!"

Another woman in a group reported that she was suffering from a type of cancer that was untreatable. In her constellation, her representative was strongly drawn towards her father and death. He had been in Hitler's SS during the war and after the war he suffered greatly from the crimes he had seen and committed in the Death's Head division. When this woman was a teenager, her father committed suicide. Here, too, the therapist attempted to find a life-supporting separation from the father and his victims, and it appeared to work with the representatives. When the client took her own place in the constellation, however, and stood in a place of resolution with her husband and children, she looked pleadingly at the therapist and begged, "Please, please, let me go to join my father." At a nod from the therapist, she lay down next to her father's representative, laughing and crying at the same time. She embraced him warmly until she slowly relaxed and became peaceful. At the end, the woman asked many questions about how to handle inheritance and other practical family issues, and it was clear that she was preparing for her death.

Representing Another

When children in a family feel that someone very close to them is being drawn into death or some difficult fate, another movement of the soul may become active. "Dear Mummy/Daddy, I will do this for you. I will die for you." It is always astounding to see the power of a movement in which one person attempts to assume the fate of another in an attempt to spare them, as if one could free someone of forces pulling them into tragedy. There are religious traditions of one person suffering for the sake of others, and religious pictures and myths that imply that one person's death can give (eternal) life to another. Sacrificing oneself for the sake of another is a driving force in the soul, reflected not only in constellations, but all around us.

In a constellation of a man suffering from cancer, we could see his mother's movement towards her own mother, who had died prematurely. The client's mother had often felt depressed, and when he was a child she had confided to him that she would much prefer to die. When the man's representative moved towards his dead grandmother, his mother's representative said, "Now I can stay with my family," and went to stand next to her husband. The client, watching the constellation from the outside, spontaneously exclaimed: "Exactly, when a woman has three children, it's better for one of the children to die than for the mother."

There was a woman who was suffering from multiple sclerosis who felt strongly drawn to her father's deceased brother. After the war, this uncle, who was then five, had been playing with his brother, the client's father, and they discovered a hand grenade. The uncle was killed when the grenade exploded. The boys' father was in a prisoner of war camp and their mother, in her grief and pain, held the elder brother responsible for her little loved one's death. She wailed, "Why wasn't it you who got hit and not my darling baby, Paul!" In the constellation, when the client was led to her father's brother, the child who had been killed, the therapist asked her to say: "Dear Uncle, I will come to you so my Daddy can live." She uttered this sentence, radiant with love. She was asked to repeat the sentence about ten times, and each time she said it with all her heart. Finally, she was startled to realise what it was that she was actually doing. She was asked to say to her uncle, "Dear Uncle, please be friendly if I live, even if that means that Daddy comes to you before his time." When she said this sentence, it was quietly, with no energy. When she returned to stand with her siblings, her father's representative felt a powerful urge to move towards his brother. The woman began to cry and, no longer able to stand alone, she sat down on the floor and buried her face in her hands. Her father took her in his arms and said, "I don't want you to suffer."

Another woman had been had committed to a psychiatric institution when she was a teenager. She was diagnosed as psychotic and although she recovered, her life remained very difficult. Relationships did not work out well for her and initial professional success gave way to many problems at work. You could feel that this woman was living at the edge of mental illness. In the constellation, it was actually her father who reacted in a crazy way. Her father, as a 16-year-old, fleeing refugee, had shot a man who was trying to rape his mother. In the constellation, the client's father was placed opposite the man he had killed and his mother, the client's grandmother. The father's representative almost went mad, and it was difficult to guide him towards a movement that would bring peace into this terrible situation. When a movement was finally found, the client felt released from the chains that had held her bound to her father and she was able to return to a place amongst her siblings. As she did so, however, a younger sister suddenly exclaimed, "Now I'm going crazy!" The client, sitting outside the constellation, heard this and screamed, "No! Then, I would rather be crazy again!"

Help, Reparations, and Fulfilment

Children are able to withstand an unbelievable amount of suffering when it is their own. It is a continual source of amazement to me what clients have had to cope with in their childhood, and how well they were able to manage it. What is extremely difficult for children, however, is to deal with the pain of someone they love. At about the age of three, a child begins to look at all those who belong to his or her family and ask, Who is this?" It is not only the people who come into view, but also their pain and suffering. The child's soul begins to carry what has become popularly known as a "life-script", in the language of Eric Berne's Transactional Analysis. This script has the effect of giving the child a voice that says, "Dear Mummy/Daddy/Sister/Granny, don't be sad. I'll help you in your pain. I am still too little, but just wait until I grow up and I'll help you." The child develops a role for life, a plan to help a loved one get free of their pain. For a child, this decision is a great relief. Later, as an adult still carrying this secret inner plan, it becomes a pattern of constraining illusion. We recognise this dynamic of the soul in many aspects of our life plans. Many of us can remember saying at some time in our childhood, "I'll never get married" or "I'm going to go and live in another country."

> The violinist Yehudi Menuhin mentioned in an interview the pain he had experienced as a child when his mother took him along looking for a place to live in New York City, and doors were repeatedly slammed in the face of poor Jews. He remembered that his reaction to his mother's despair had been his decision to become so famous that no one could ever slam the door on a member of his family.

> A paediatrician came to a group, completely burned out. He owned and ran a private children's clinic, where he worked practically day and night and was very successful. However, his wife and children had turned away from him and his health was collapsing under the stress. During a guided fantasy, a repressed memory surfaced of himself as a five-year-old boy clinging to his mother's knees and crying, "Oh, Mummy, I'll make it up to you!" He had been playing with his brother and had given him a shove that unintentionally caused the boy to fall from a bridge to his death.

The soul dynamic that says, "I will help relieve your pain," comes from children's empathy and their sense of unbearable helplessness in the face of family events. This is a powerful, moving force in our lives that can be utilised in a positive way if, with maturation, we shed the attendant illusion. We are destined to fail, however, if our efforts remain entangled with that earlier pain that belonged to someone else, pain which that person has already suffered, or pain that has long since disappeared.

We encounter family themes that are based on such "secret life plans" in fairy tales, fiction, films, plays, operas, and so on, which have an emotional impact on us throughout the course of our lives. In constellations, we see these dynamics when children move to their parents or loved ones, filled with strength and great love, and take the adults in their arms to comfort them, as if it were the children who were big and all-powerful (Schneider and Gross, 2000).

We see similar dynamics when, following the premature death of a loved one, an internal voice says, "I will live your life to its proper ending. I will live for you as well as myself." We sometimes then work "for two", or lead a "double" life, we might even take up some profession with no apparent reason, unaware that this was the profession of an excluded family member.

It is not only the loss of the loved one in the family that is difficult to bear; we can hardly stand to see a life unfulfilled as desired because of a premature death or because of some difficult fate, such as an incapacitating impairment. We leap into the breach with all the love and determination of our child's soul. In addition to living our own lives, we attempt to use our energy to fulfil that other, interrupted life, as if we could bring it to completion in this way.

Horror and Atrocity

Every day in the media, we are confronted by the horrors and atrocities of life, and the images of suffering seem to hold a strange fascination for us. At the scene of an accident, passers-by are drawn to stare as they move past, and newspapers count on pictures of tragedy and suffering to draw our attention. Normally, however, we remain at some distance, unless we have personally and directly witnessed some terrible event.

What happens, however, when terrible things are experienced tangibly in the family? A boy who runs through a post-war meadow and steps on a land mine, blowing his leg off, will experience a terrible, personal trauma. The physical body will do everything possible to cope with the pain and survive, and if the child gets the necessary assistance, he will continue life with one leg as best he can. What happens, however, if that child is running behind his mother and she is the one to step on the mine and have her leg blown off? What happens to the child? How can he hear the screams of his mother, see the blood and the dismembered leg, and cope with his horror, his empathetic suffering, and his helplessness?

Those terrible images will remain long beyond the actual situation, and the boy will need to make a great effort to repress the sounds and images. To free ourselves of horrible impressions that continue to work in our memories and torture our souls, we often have to go so far as to suppress our love towards the person who suffered the atrocity. Loving that person brings the terrible images and pain to the surface again. This is why family members who have had a horrible accident or have died in some atrocious way are often shut out of memory and out of the flow of love, sometimes extending over many generations. When they are mentioned, it is often with a cold, distant quality. It is not rare that a later family member will develop mental or physical symptoms that point towards the unfortunately afflicted person, sometimes with astonishing precision. In any event, it is a dynamic that appears repeatedly in constellations.

A woman came to a group because of major problems with her five-year-old daughter. When things didn't go her way, this child threw herself on the floor, screaming and kicking her legs wildly. In these situations, there was no way to calm her down. Her mother often felt helpless in the face of these outbursts and she would end up screaming at the child or slapping her to bring her back to her senses. The mother was suffering enormously from these repeated battles with her daughter. In the constellation, representatives for the mother and her daughter were placed facing one another. The mother seemed cold and distant, and the daughter's representative began to sway; her eyes opened wide as she fell to the floor, kicking her legs wildly. She screamed and rolled around the floor holding her hands over her ears. Finally she crawled under a chair. Her reaction was so powerful that she had to be taken out of the role and helped to calm down.

The client was asked if that scene reminded her of anything. She told a story about what had happened to her father during the war. He had belonged to a commando that was laying land mines in the path of the advancing Russian soldiers. Her father was very afraid of getting hurt in this dangerous job and, in fact, he eventually did step on a mine and lost both his legs. Later, with the help of prostheses, he was able to walk again. He married and had six children, and was able to work and provide for his family.

The client was the youngest of the children and her father's favourite. She said when she was about six something happened that made her love for her father evaporate into thin air. He showed her his artificial legs and told her the story of what had happened to him. As a teenager, she was in constant conflict with her father and even later, she would do anything rather than what he wanted her to do. She was living abroad when he died and she had not able to talk to him.

Now the woman had these problems with her daughter, and the child's representative in the constellation was behaving in a way that brought up the memory of that accident. Coincidentally, the client had chosen a representative who had also lost a leg in a car accident. No one knew this, since the woman was wearing prosthesis under a long skirt. What was going on here? There is no way we can know exactly. It appears that as a child, when the client was suddenly made fully aware of her father's disability and with the story of the incident, she could imagine that terrible war scene. We could guess that the child's only way to cope with this was by closing off her love for her father. Her own daughter was now leading the woman back to her father's fate and confronting her with her own child-like helplessness.

In the constellation, the woman was placed facing her father and they had a dialogue that retroactively calmed the horror of the little girl back then, sitting on her father's lap. As an adult in the constellation, she was able to sort things out with her father about how she had behaved and the decisions she had made. She then was able to say goodbye to him with love and a great feeling of relief.

When there have been terrible deaths in a family, the memories are often suffused with recriminations as well. We tend to hold our loved ones responsible for their accidents. We cannot tolerate our feelings of helplessness and our recriminations suggest that if the person who was killed had been more careful, it wouldn't have happened. In cases of accidental death, there are also consequences for other family members.

In a supervision group, a therapist asked to work on a personal problem. Her left leg was in a plaster cast and she said she had just broken that leg for the third time within a very short period of time. She felt she could not continue doing therapy work until she understood the meaning of these accidents. The therapist initially did not want to address this issue, but he became convinced that the woman was taking this very seriously. The constellation began with two representatives, the woman and her injured leg. The woman's representative tried to get away from the leg, but the leg held on to her, lovingly, but very persistently. Representatives were added for the woman's mother and father. The leg representative went over to the woman's mother and clung to her. Although she too wanted to get away from it, the leg was right behind her all the time. Representatives were added for the mother's parents. Now, the leg representative moved to the grandfather, who accepted it lovingly. In response, the woman and her mother both moved to the grandfather and tearfully embraced him. Only the grandmother turned away. The therapist-client watched the scene silently with tears in her eyes. Then she said, "Of course, now I remember. My grandfather had a motorcycle accident when my mother was three years old. His left leg was so damaged that the doctors wanted to amputate it, but my grandfather refused. His leg didn't heal and he became bedridden. Eventually, he got cancer in the leg and died, ten years after the accident. My mother's experience of her father during her childhood was distant and strange. After my grandfather's accident, my grandmother became very depressed. My mother left home as soon as it was feasible."

When someone in a family is involved in a major, catastrophic event, such as a war or disaster, the survivors are often left under the spell of the horror. The reality that invades the senses is unbearable. Films portraying the persecution of the Jews and the atrocities of the concentration camps often make the viewer feel disturbed by the coldness of Jewish victims towards the suffering of their own people. However, in such a battle for personal survival, how could anyone bear the additional burden of empathy with others? Those who escape and survive can rarely look back. It would be like Job's daughter being turned to stone. Turning away, however, even for the sake of survival, may have terrible consequences. The traumatisation narrows the range of feelings and behaviour and the flow of love. It is not only what one has suffered personally that intrudes into awareness and demands healing and some kind of real ending; those who have died horribly also force their way back into memories. It seems that those who come later have to recall these shut out "ghosts" so that something can be done to give them a place in the hearts of the survivors and their descendents and to release them from their catastrophe and finally grant them peace in death.

A Brazilian woman came to an individual session because of problems with her husband and children. She did a constellation using figures, in which it was immediately clear that something much deeper was involved. Her parents, both Jews who had been in concentration camps as teenagers, had survived the war and later married. They ended up in Brazil, where their children were born. No one in her father's family died in the concentration camps, but everyone in her mother's family was killed.

The therapist added a row of figures for the members of the mother's family and placed two figures for the woman and her mother facing the others. When the client was asked what movement her mother might want to make, she tearfully moved the figure representing her mother over to the group of her family members. For the first time, she consciously looked at all those who had been murdered, and for the first time, she felt a deep empathy with her mother and recognised her mother's powerful desire to join the dead. Her mother had never spoken a word about her concentration camp experience or about her family. One could imagine that this mother was, in some way, not really present and was probably unable to allow herself to have strong feelings of love for her children, as a mechanism for holding the unspoken pain at bay. The children, however, felt resentful of their mother.

Some time after the session, the woman visited her mother in Israel and her mother told her, for the first time, about her experiences in the Holocaust. The woman also discovered that, coincidentally, on the afternoon she was looking at her mother's murdered family for the first time in the constellation, her mother was telling her story for the first time in her life, to the film director Steven Spielberg. It is strange how events sometimes happen in a synchronistic way. As this mother lay on her deathbed, her children came from their various homes all over the world to be with her.

Justice: The Rewards and the Price

There is a deep-seated need for justice and balance in the soul. Consciously, this appears in various forms, such as a balance of giving and taking in relationships, as debt, as guilt and repayment, and as reparation. We feel it as a need for revenge and atonement. We sense imbalances and injustices in our conscience and feel a need to bring relationships into order by correcting the imbalance and acting in fair and just ways. We also avoid a feeling of imbalance in terms of good luck or happiness in close relationships. For example, when one partner wakes up in the morning and declares that he or she slept very badly during the night, the other partner may reply with a comment about also not having slept well, even if this is not true.

Constellation work in many different cultures has confirmed that we are subject to movements of relationship systems, conscious or unconscious, that seek to maintain balance. It appears that the cohesiveness of the group is jeopardised if one member has too much good fortune and another not enough. It is as if a law of entropy operating in the soul were to draw life and order into death and disruption, tearing at the orders of life and success and bringing failure and death. It is impossible to bring someone back from the dead, but it is certainly possible for us to die.

When someone has profited in the course of their life and fate at a high cost to someone else's life and fate, the beneficiary of the gain will often unconsciously attempt to even things up by paying the original price again. This is the kind of pressure felt by a child whose mother died at the child's birth, by a second wife whose husband killed his first wife, by someone who has inherited a large estate that came into the family through injustice or exploitation of others, by a new boss who has got the position because the previous boss was driven out by harassment. Such a movement towards reparation often extends over generations.

During a course in Mexico, a young Mexican man asked to do a constellation. The therapist had noticed that this man was often chosen as a representative and always fell to the floor with a radiant look on his face. There was always some correlation to the basic dynamics in the constellations, but it seemed overly dramatic. The constellations were done on a stage, which meant that people had to go up a few stairs to get to the working space. As the young man leapt up the stairs, he tripped and fell flat out on his face. He beamed, nonetheless, as he picked himself up and came to sit next to the therapist. The therapist looked at him and said, "You're a regular kamikaze!" The man was startled. The therapist added, "and you live dangerously." The young man shook his head and said that was not at all true. His girlfriend, sitting in the audience, interrupted, saying, "Of course you live dangerously. You drive your car so fast that I have refused to ride with you a couple of times." In the ensuing interview, it emerged that the young man had a hangglider and had crashed twice, both times without serious injury. The therapist looked at the man and mentioned that he also looked Japanese, not Mexican.

The young man told the following story: His grandfather was actually Japanese, and as a sixteen-year-old during the war he had volunteered as a Kamikaze pilot, the suicide commandos that flew their planes into the targets to ensure precision for their bomb load. When the great-grandfather heard about his son's actions, he packed him off to Mexico to keep him safe. There, the grandfather then later married a Japanese woman and their daughter was the young man's mother. It was not clear whether his mother had married a Japanese man or a Mexican, but the young man looked very Japanese.

The therapist asked a representative to take the role of one of the kamikaze pilots who had sacrificed their lives for their country, and to lie down on the floor. He placed representatives for the great-grandfather, the grandfather, and the young man in front of the pilot. The dead kamikaze pilot was so filled with rage that he was shaking. The grandfather turned away and moved off several steps. The great-grandfather tried to attend to the pilot, but this only increased his fury. The great-grandfather looked around helplessly and then he too moved away. The client's representative smiled broadly and lay down next to the pilot. This reflects the dynamic at the level of the soul. The grandfather had been rescued at a cost to his country and a kind of "betrayal" towards the other kamikaze pilots. It seemed as though the young man could only take the gift of his life if he also died (probably with his hangglider).

When asked, the young man said that he had not yet been to Japan. The therapist suggested that the man go to visit the land of his ancestors and seek out a memorial to the kamikaze pilots. He should put flowers at this memorial and silently tell those pilots that he respected their sacrifice and, in view of what they had done, he would cherish his own life. The therapist also suggested that the young man might do something that benefited Japan in some way. In the constellation, the pilot found a peaceful place when he was in the arms of a representative of Japan and when the three men had bowed before the pilot and country. The young man was very serious and thoughtful as he returned to his seat.

In the introduction to this book, I briefly mentioned a moving example of a Brazilian man whose Indian mother was sent away by his father when the child was two. In that constellation, the mother's deep suffering for her lost child was very moving. The Brazilian man came to the group with his wife because their marriage was in trouble as a consequence of the man's professional difficulties. The man was the son of a successful businessman, and had taken over one of the two family businesses. He ran the business successfully, but one day there was an electrical short circuit and the business burnt to the ground. It was insufficiently insured, so he was ruined. His father then retired and turned over the second business to his son. The son also ran this business well but, as if cursed, this business burnt to the ground as well, though the cause was never discovered. The man lost everything for the second time. His father had died before this event, and all the man's inheritance had gone into this business. At the time of the constellation, the man had a small shop that he ran with the help of his wife. Even with great effort they could earn only a subsistence living for themselves and their children.

The constellation began with the man and his wife and then was expanded to include his father and mother and finally, also representatives of the two businesses. In contrast to the very moving but static constellation regarding his mother's loss, this constellation took on a rather astonishing direction when the businesses were added. The representative of the first business lay near the mother's representative and snuggled up to her like a little child.

When asked about any prior relationships of his father's, the man said that his father had had a previous wife and two sons. He did not know what had happened to them and he didn't know his two brothers, nor had he ever had any contact with them. His father's first wife and two sons were added to the constellation. The representative of the second business spontaneously moved to the first family, stood behind them and put his arms around the three.

Such processes seem curious and rather eerie. It is as if coincidence and systemic needs are working together to bring balance, without regard for the actual consequences for the people involved. The client's father had acted unjustly on two occasions. He had sent his son's mother away and prevented contact between them, and he had shut out his first two sons and disinherited them. His youngest, favourite son got all the wealth his father had amassed, but he couldn't keep it. His mother and his two brothers had paid too high a price. The "gain" of the accursed two businesses was burnt to ashes and the man suffered the same kind of loss as those before him. In the constellation, the man was led to his mother and taken in her arms like a small child. All his pent-up pain poured out, and his mother could finally express her love. The man's tears seemed practically endless as his mother beamed and comforted her child. His wife wept as well, but with her eyes open, and with love for her husband and his mother. The man also faced his two brothers at the end of the constellation and they, too, took him sympathetically in their arms. The two businesses, however, pulled back to the edge of the constellation. The man's father also had tears in his eyes as he bowed his head, in contrast to his previous proud posture. He approached his son and embraced him and then went to stand with his two businesses.

When there is an issue involving a loss or repeated failure in life that seems inexplicable, it is often useful to look into the family system for someone who has paid a very high price in some way. Such a fate in one person's life makes it difficult for others in the system to live their own lives fully and to completely accept and enjoy their own good luck.

Consider a situation in which a man's ex-fiancée committed suicide when he left her. What is the effect on his later wife and children? Regardless of whether they know anything about the other woman's death or the reasons behind it, the wife owes her marriage and the children their lives to the fact that the man did not marry his earlier fiancée. If the separation had no serious, painful consequences, the later debt does not carry much weight, but what happens when the consequences were serious? Regardless of any cause and effect relationship, the soul connects these fates in such a way that the suicide of the fiancée weighs in as the "price" of the later family's "gain". Later family members attempt to reduce the pressure that has been created by an imbalance between the price paid and the profit gained, by restoring balance in some way. The fiancée cannot be brought back to life, but it is still possible to reduce or eliminate the gain. In some situations like this, a later wife might allow her marriage to fail and "give up" her husband. Or, a daughter of the later marriage may seek out a partner that leaves her. Such a daughter may spend her whole life alone, or have suicidal tendencies, or perhaps even commit suicide. It is unlikely that it would occur to anyone that there could be any connection to the man's previous fiancée, because these disastrous, compensating movements take place unconsciously and are systemic compensations, not personal ones.

> In one group, there was a German artist who lived in an isolated cabin in the woods in Italy. He was just barely able to live on a small amount of governmental assistance, and he seemed haunted, like someone on the run. The man's father, before his death, had told his son about his war experience in Italy, in the same province where the son now lived. The father had been given orders to hunt down deserters and shoot them on the spot.
>
> The constellation consisted of three representatives: the father, the son, and a deserter. The desperate deserter kept trying, unsuccessfully,

to hide from the father. To the father's dismay, his son lay down next to the deserter. The son now, in reality, was hiding in his Italian cabin, just as the deserters had done. The man's art brought him neither income nor success. He was living exactly like a deserter on the run.

Another man in a group had never had a real relationship with a woman, had never really had a profession, was often ill, and had attempted suicide several times. Shortly before coming to the constellation group, he had done some research into his family history and discovered that he was actually Jewish. His mother's parents were Jews who had managed to falsify their ancestry and thus survived the war. Even when the danger had passed, the Jewish family history remained a secret. This man, however, felt unaccountably drawn to Judaism and in the constellation he experienced a painful but freeing connection to the Jews who were murdered.

At a certain level, the soul attends to a balance and justice, but blindly and impersonally. This is particularly apparent in the fates of victims and perpetrators. As I have already mentioned, in the families of victims as well as the families of perpetrators, we often observe later family members (usually grandchildren or great-grandchildren) representing these earlier victims or perpetrators. When events touch life or death issues, survival, or the basic fundamentals of our existence, victims and perpetrators are bound together in their experience, even though they may not wish to be and may be unable to see it. This bond is forged during the actual event and is not dependent upon personal guilt or responsibility. It is naturally difficult for those involved or their children to acknowledge a connection like this, so the victims or perpetrators are excluded from awareness. Later, the collective conscience forces descendents to represent these excluded individuals, often pushing them in some way to live out the fate of someone who has been excluded from the family memory. It is as if this is the only path towards reconciliation that acknowledges the bond between the victims and perpetrators.

In constellations, we have noticed that the strongest pull towards this kind of representation comes from victims and perpetrators who were personally in contact with one another. Politicians or oppressors operating from behind a desk in the background, without actual physical contact with their victims, do not seem to affect the later generations of their victims in the same way as those perpetrators who had close physical contact in the injury, damage, or death of their victims. This direct expression of hate-filled, cold-blooded, murderous energy seems to carry the most weight in the soul of an individual or family in terms of later representation, and seemingly regardless of any political or social context, or "objective" justifications.

Even people involved with one another in a traffic accident remain bound together in some way. Again, the critical influential factors are whether there are deaths or serious consequences. Personal guilt may exacerbate the dynamics present, but is of no real consequence in terms of the bonds that are forged. Advances in technology and medicine have increased opportunities for gain and loss (for example in the area of organ transplants), and fate is increasingly influenced by human intervention. The more we consider individuals or groups responsible for our fate, and the more our gains and losses extend out into societal networks (as is the case with increasing globalisation), the wider the reach of this compensatory movement in the soul.

The Dead Are Present Among Us

Most constellations involve issues of life and death. There is hardly a family in which some member or members have not died prematurely, or in a way that seemed inappropriate. Our soul seems to place a high value on a dignified and respectful parting with the dead. It is clear in wartime, how much effort and energy are exerted to ensure the retrieval and proper burial of the dead. In Europe, one can see the great number of cemeteries established after the war for the fallen soldiers. All this is easy to understand from the point of view of the living, but it is more difficult to entertain the idea that the dead are aware of their death and also need to take leave of the living. We actually don't know anything about the dead, and in constellations they are represented by living people, who naturally cannot actually represent the reality of being dead. But representatives can feel the effects in the souls of the living, and the soul binds the living and the dead beyond the actual event of dying. Representatives of the dead often behave in surprising ways, and sometimes bring a kind of energy into a constellation that makes us consider the idea that there may be more powerful forces at work here than we normally assume when we think about the dead.

A core issue in constellation work arises whenever deceased members of the system have been excluded from the memory and love of the living, or situations in which a death has left something unfinished, or where those surviving are still ill at ease. The dead souls then seem to be excluded and not at peace. We might ask who has died so suddenly in this family that their souls are still clinging to the living, as if they were not yet dead? These are dynamics that encumber the process of dying.

When there are deceased family members who are not yet at peace in the family soul, and therefore continue to affect the living as if they were still alive, the constellation work often resembles a shamanic ritual. Through the representatives, the living and the dead are able to meet, but it also seems to be that the dead can touch others who are dead. Such encounters seem to release the dead from haunting the living in their search for peace. It allows love to flow in the hearts of the living and, insofar as we can say such a thing, love also flows between the dead, and from the dead to the living. When the soul connections are intact, the dead can be dead and the living can live. In a film about healers in Nepal, a medicine man was asked who went to medical doctors in his area, and who went to healers? In his opinion, those who are ill in an ordinary way go to doctors, and those who cannot find peace with someone who has died come to a healer.

In constellations, the living and the dead have an opportunity to say goodbye in a way that was perhaps impossible in reality. Many of the dead seem to need some sign of peace and release from the living, and many of those still alive need some assurance of release from a person who has died. There appear to be dead people who have to be reminded that they are dead before they can let go of the living. Often the dead can only find peace when they are allowed to lie in peace next to others who are also dead, for example a mother who died prematurely, or a twin who died at birth, a first love, a murderer, or perhaps a fallen comrade.

> There was a woman in a group who was the sole survivor of four siblings. Two brothers and one sister had died at birth before she was born. In the constellation, the woman looked calmly at her dead siblings lying together on the floor. Her mother wept for her two sons, but the father seemed cut off from his wife's grief and from his children, as if he had to shut out the pain and simply declare that "life must go on". Strangely enough, the mother was only concerned about her sons, and no one seemed to feel anything for the daughter who had died. When the representative of this child was asked, she said, "I'm not dead at all," and stood up. The therapist assured her that she was, indeed, dead, but she looked at her parents and living sister with lively curiosity and declared, "I am clearly alive."

The therapist brought in a representative for a doctor and placed him facing the sister. He looked at her for a while and then said, "I'm afraid I have to take your life again. The way you look, you won't survive long and it will only be a shock to your parents." The baby, who was supposedly born dead, then said, "Well, if that is the way it is, I'll just lie down on the floor again," and she lay down and closed her eyes. Her mother and living sister went to her, weeping, and held her in their arms in love and pain.

We do not have any way of knowing what happened at this child's birth. Perhaps the baby was not dead at birth, but only severely handicapped. The only thing we know is the feeling of peace that suddenly came over this family in the constellation when the doctor spoke these words aloud, and how helpful it felt when something was allowed to finish. The client, who had previously seemed rather cold and brittle, felt very relaxed and radiated a sense of heartfelt warmth.

When I served as a representative for a young victim of the Argentine Junta, I discovered that I was less concerned with the suffering I had to undergo than with the fact that, although I had died, no one was aware of it. There were two things that really touched me and kept me from finding peace. One was that I had not been able to say goodbye to my mother properly, and the other was that the public outcry of the mothers of Buenos Aires made it impossible for my family to mourn for me. I wanted a grave with my family. I would have been so happy to "see" my family standing by my grave with flowers and warm and cheerful faces. I was rather disturbed by the public discussion and the attempts of all these mothers to uncover my fate and the fate of others who had disappeared. I was at peace with the idea of being dead and being acknowledged as such and I imagined my family and friends coming to visit my grave now and again and so letting me continue to participate in their lives a bit. Whatever part my own personal beliefs played in such a role, I was able to experience something of what leave-taking means to both the living and the dead.

The Resolving Forces of the Soul

The strong bonds in the soul have a constant and lasting systemic effect that ensures that the family stays intact, with each member granted an equal right to a place. This bonding for wholeness extends to the relationship of the living to their ancestors. Wherever and whenever imbalance is created, there is a movement elsewhere to re-establish balance. Events cause disruptions in our lives when the soul cannot process it fast enough, and there is a force that pushes towards repetition. Family members who come later, although they were not originally involved, are nonetheless called into "service" to balance out, or in some way complete the disasters of the past, and to put an end to whatever has remained unfinished in the family system. This is the core of entanglements that severely limit our autonomy.

Family constellations serve primarily to give us insight into these strange systemic processes. They strive for "aha" experiences that directly affect clients, and often indirectly affect the person's family. They allow someone to "see" events in a way that he or she can say, "Now things make sense to me."

Beyond this function, however, constellations seek paths that allow the strength of our spirit and soul to put an end to earlier misfortunes and to be free to meet the sufferings and satisfactions of our current lives. This requires an explicit acknowledgement that I belong to my parents and my family, with all their suffering, their guilt, and their debts, and an awareness of the fact that I am subject to the turns of fate and helpless to control them. The next step is differentiating between what belongs to fate and what is the responsibility of my parents and other family members. The loving connections remain, but blind love can be replaced by face-to-face, conscious love that binds but at the same time can also let go. We have to take in the effects of entanglements, but we can learn to distinguish between the effects and those aspects that lie within our personal responsibility. For example, descendents of Nazis are not personally responsible for the deeds of their forefathers, but they still have to live with the consequences of those actions. In the end, it takes a "constructive" process to resolve the terrible impressions stored in the unconscious of the system. A constructed image paves the way for the future, but it also affects what lies in the past. Memories and remembrance can be actively altered to allow us to forget without repression, and to accept reality with love.

Reclaiming the Excluded

I recently received a letter from a woman who had been in a group some years earlier, telling me what had happened afterwards. In the constellation it had emerged that a sibling was missing, probably a child from her father's previous relationship. The woman asked her father if that was true and he admitted it was possible. A former girlfriend of his from Switzerland had once written to him that she was pregnant, but said she did not want him to have any contact with the child. He had never followed up on her claim. The client couldn't let it go, so with her sister's help, she located her half-brother. The result was that the whole family, including her father, now had contact with this man, and her parents' relationship had changed for the better. Her father was more open and was also really taking care of his health. The client had previously been in a relationship with a man that was like a brother-sister relationship, but she had moved on and was now in love with someone else.

Things do not necessarily turn out well when excluded members are seen and integrated into the family. Often, you can already see in the constellation that the system is not ready to open up to the excluded members. The therapist can try to find whatever is needed to break the ice. This is like a test of what is missing in the system and what is needed in order to be able to take in those who have been excluded. Perhaps there is a forgotten sibling who died at birth who needs to be taken into the arms of the family, given a place in their hearts, mourned, and bid adieu. Perhaps a father needs to say to his wife, "You are not to blame. I will carry the burden with you," so that a child that has died suddenly can be given a place again. Perhaps a man needs to acknowledge a former fiancée as his first partner so that she can let go of her anger towards him and his later family. An illegitimate child who had no contact with his or her grandparents may need to visit the grandfather's grave later.

The therapist helps the client and family open their hearts to those who have been excluded so that all who belong can come together again, even if it is at a graveside. If actual contact is possible, the soul seems to prefer a real meeting as well, but this is not always possible, and it is not always easy. Sometimes representatives or clients resist efforts or suggestions from the therapist. A therapist cannot make resolution happen. Resolution can only arise from the soul of the system when truth has comes to light and reintegration becomes possible, opening up new paths for relationships. Knowing about each other and having contact, if that is possible, loosen the bonds of fate and connections become clearer and more flexible.

Grieving for the Dead and Letting Them Go

In burial rites in the jungles of Thailand, far from civilisation, it is reportedly the custom to take the dead body on a stretcher and carry it in a procession to a far distant place. There, the corpse is burned and the ashes put in an urn. The urn is secured in that place and the community returns to their village to begin a year of mourning. When the year comes to an end, a festive procession returns to the location and the urn is carried back to the village to be buried with relatives. A great celebration marks the end of the process.

This is a good description of what our soul needs when someone close to us has died. The first step is letting go of the dead person. This person is dead and the physical relationship is at an end. Pain and grief are appropriate reactions to this ending. After a time, which cannot be overly long, the mourning must stop. The dead one comes near again as an ancestor and has a place in the hearts of the living. There is a celebration of the union of the living and the dead in service to life.

Many people have difficulty letting go of the deceased, and others cannot take them into their hearts. Constellations provide an opportunity for both these processes to be completed. It is very moving experience, particularly for someone who has lost a parent. Children are often unable to grieve because the pain is too overwhelming for them, and adult forms of mourning may make children fearful or leave them feeling isolated. Sometimes a system is carrying an additional burden of guilt (or perhaps even feelings of relief if there were bitter rows between the parents, or if death was preceded by a long, incurable illness). Grieving can be completed in a constellation when obstacles are revealed, and natural pain and love are allowed to flow. If the constellation ends in relief and joy for everyone in the group, it is clear that the process of grieving has been successfully completed. It is difficult to describe the depth with which a group can follow someone else's grief process in a constellation and how enriching the experience is for everyone. This process can also be supported through a guided fantasy.

> A woman was severely depressed following the death of her son. The official version was that he had killed himself, but he had been involved in the drug scene and his mother was convinced that he had been murdered. Following repeated appeals, his body was exhumed, but there was no reliable proof of what had happened. She was left with her uncertainty and fell into a serious depression. The therapist deemed a constellation inappropriate in her situation, so he asked her to close her eyes and look at her son in her mind's eye, and to see him just the way she loved him. Then, she was asked to let her son slowly move away into the background behind her. The woman began to weep quietly with her head bowed low. Slowly, over a period of many minutes, she raised her head until she was again sitting upright. Her face was noticeably lighter, and when she opened her eyes she said, "Now I know what it means to put the dead behind you."

Leaving Illusion Behind

I have already mentioned how we fall prey to our illusions in our childlike empathy and our childish fantasies of unlimited power. These fantasies make us feel as if sacrificing our life could prevent terrible things from happening, or might rescue someone, or make somebody else happy. After the initial euphoria of the resolution in a constellation, clients sometimes fall back into a feeling of depression or disappointment when they realise fully how much their lives have been determined by fruitless love, and how they have done damage to themselves without having helped their parents or loved ones. That is a difficult realisation to bear. The relief of the constellation can only be integrated by a deep acceptance of what is without illusion. When we are free of our illusions many of our choices, efforts, and old habits collapse. What is to fill this empty space? Although we maintain that we want a fulfilled life, we may actually avoid solutions because they present us with new challenges, forcing us into open, loving contact with the misfortunes of others. Resolution also leaves us with an unfilled gap in our feelings and thoughts, a space that has to be filled with something new and unknown.

> There was a woman who had repeatedly chosen men who turned out to have alcohol problems. In her father's family, the parents and all the children except her father were alcoholics. Predictably, he looked down on his family, feeling proud of his superiority, and broke off all contact with them. In the constellation, the woman reconnected to her father's family and there was a great, joyful greeting. Afterwards, the woman seemed very happy and free, but the next day she felt terrible again. She became fully aware of the magnitude of the suffering in her father's family and in her own failed relationships, in which she had invested so much effort and hope. She felt empty and unsettled. Later, however, a calm settled over her and she felt a new sense of strength. She visited her father's brothers and sisters who were still alive, undertook the care of a neglected aunt, changed to a better paying job, and cautiously began a new relationship with a man.

The illusions so necessary for a child must be adjusted to match reality in adulthood. What is needed for the adult is an acceptance of life, however it has actually been up to now. An adult must develop a mature love for his or her parents to look ahead to the future. A therapist can help the process of adjusting childhood illusions by resisting any urge to guide a constellation towards illusory solutions that leave terrible events or family conflicts unseen and unacknowledged. Sometimes therapists feel as though they have to find a good resolution for everyone in the constellation at any price. That only supports a client's illusions of all-powerful importance. The only thing that truly helps is to allow the constellation to confront the client with the reality of life and responsibility. A constellation cannot move to any resolution beyond the reality that the family system allows.

Reconciliation

Ultimately, all therapy is a process of reconciliation. It is a process of consciousness-raising and integrating previously split-off parts of the self and, consequently, splits between people. It brings reconciliation between the illusions of childhood and the true meaning of events. This is extremely difficult when children have been seriously injured by their parents, or perhaps have even been given away. It is difficult when partners have caused each other harm or physical or mental distress. It is particularly challenging when someone is seeking reconciliation between victims and perpetrators, or peace in the aftermath of war.

Representatives are very sensitive to these tensions, even when they are open to a process of reconciliation. What is needed, first of all, for victim or perpetrator, is to name the violation and to acknowledge what has been suffered or what has been done. If this is done carelessly, with empty words or gestures, the movement towards reconciliation will almost always be rejected.

For clients, representatives, and therapists, it is a powerful experience to seek, and hopefully to find, the right words, gestures, and movements in a constellation with victims and perpetrators. Not every constellation, however, opens a path towards reconciliation. Sometimes, it seems as though the time is not ripe for such a movement. In Poland, for example, I experienced a deeply moving openness to reconciliation when it came to the war, the Holocaust, issues of expulsion and exile, and other devastating events from that particular period of history. It was much more difficult, however, to find any opening for reconciliation when we were confronting the events of the communist regime.

In the early days of constellation work, perpetrators were often sent out of the room as a symbol that they had lost their right to belong to the group because of their actions, and to make clear that later members of the system would not have to exclude themselves as compensation.

Over time, it has become clear that this procedure does not lead to a deep release for the descendents of victims or perpetrators. It has become ever clearer that the perpetrators and victims are drawn to one another and that there is an inseparable bond between them. An attempt to exclude the perpetrators only strengthens this bond. They have easier access to feelings of empathy with their victims when the victim-perpetrator connection is recognised, and when there is some awareness of their mutuality in the face of death, or "the greater soul". We have increasingly recognised the need for a movement that acknowledges perpetrators' as well as victims' entitlement to a place in the family or societal system. It is only then that perpetrators seem able to open up to any awareness of their deeds and feelings of empathy with their victims. The most difficult question in the process of reconciliation is how to deal with perpetrators in a way that opens up a path to peace and reconciliation not only between victims and perpetrators, but also for their descendents in later generations.

> A woman in a group felt a sense of panic at the thought that her father was a murderer because he was an influential engineer in the building of the V2 rocket. The therapist asked ten representatives to lie next to each other on the floor to represent the citizens of England who had lost their lives in the bomb attacks of V2 rockets. Then he added a representative for the woman's father and placed him facing the dead. As he stood there, he felt completely cold and untouched. After a while, the therapist asked the English representatives how they felt. One said, "I have nothing to do with him," and another commented, "What a pity we didn't have that rocket first." None of the ten attributed any blame to this man. Then, the father could really look at the dead and tears came to his eyes.

> A man's grandfather had come to Munich from Austria in order to serve as a policeman under Hitler. When he was placed opposite his probable victims, he felt unmoved and the dead on the floor edged away from him. The therapist added a representative for Hitler and had the grandfather say to him, "I did all of this for you." Hitler's representative smiled at first and said that was fine. Then he scornfully said, "I really couldn't care less." The grandfather, with a sense of being a victim as well, could then lie down next to his victims. He breathed deeply and said, "For the first time I can feel something. This is a good place for me. This is where I belong." His victims were able to accept this.

Reconciliation only carries weight when it is not just an easy apology on the part of the perpetrator, and when it is not a case of the victim granting forgiveness from a position of moral superiority. Such forgiveness would be a monstrous presumption, an abasement of the perpetrator, and demeaning to the victims. Finding a path to reconciliation is a challenge because we are dealing with guilt, terrible consequences, and our own helplessness. Forgiveness is not the answer; what helps is for perpetrators and victims to carry the consequences of the terrible deeds so that in time the deeds and their consequences can come to an end. Perpetrators must be protected from acts of revenge, and the reckoning must be left to death, that greater force that treats everyone the same. Cain was forced to leave his family when he murdered his brother, Abel, but he was given the mark of Cain on his forehead as a sign that he was a murderer and under God's protection. No one was allowed to do anything to him.

Reconciliation can be supported when there is an acknowledgement that a perpetrator acted in the way that was open to him or her, and also the acknowledgement that there was nothing the victim could have done to avoid that harmful event. Fate brought this victim and this perpetrator together to a degree that is often beyond the responsibility of any single perpetrator or victim. Guilt or innocence is sometimes determined only by the circumstances of our lives. Innocence is often more a gift than an achievement, and reconciliation is larger than individual effort. It entails yielding to a greater power that eventually (at the latest in death) puts victims and perpetrators on an equal footing, perhaps even with equal warmth. This is only possible if we envision the cosmos as one, filled with love that includes all people and all of creation. Even the most evil perpetrators are still human beings and in many religions are still entitled to last rites or prayers. In view of the magnitude and atrocity of some of the crimes committed, this reflects a deep humility, but also represents an opportunity for humankind.

Reconciliation between the descendents of victims and perpetrators is perhaps most durable when they are able to mourn together for the dead on both sides and hold all in respectful memory. In the soul, the deceased victims and the deceased perpetrators need the love of the living long after the actual events. One consequence of the deeds that have been perpetrated is that victims and perpetrators can only be loved in conjunction with each other. If a perpetrator had many victims on his or her conscience, it may be more than the love of a single person can carry. Resolution may only be possible through the love of many, that is, at a societal level. We get some idea of this movement in some of Bert Hellinger's large presentations when hundreds of people have been deeply moved by the process of constellations involving victims and perpetrators at a societal level.

Justice Forgone and Appropriate Compensation

Injustice and guilt demand compensation, whether or not the actions were freely chosen. Individual responsibility or circumstances carry little weight in terms of the demands of the greater soul. An individual who causes damage, however innocently, still feels the need to make amends. Everyone who personally causes injustice is responsible for it and has to compensate in some way.

Some injustice and guilt, of course, can never be atoned for by individuals or even by larger groups. There are events that can never be made good in reality. A person who murders another can never make up for that or compensate adequately. Even if the murderer commits suicide, it doesn't really change anything for the victims. The only action that would make up for it would be to bring the dead back to life or to undo the act that was done, and neither is possible. To resolve serious conflicts between people, we need compensation whenever possible, but reconciliation requires that we forgo justice in cases where pursuing "justice" simply engenders more injustice. "An eye for an eye and a tooth for a tooth" does not cancel out damage; it doubles it. A negative compensation might satisfy some need for revenge or atonement, but it does not truly bring peace. So, what remains to us in the way of meaningful compensation?

There are some cases in which it is possible to make up for harm or to give something that balances the scales of justice. Leniency is appropriate when an injustice is minor enough that forgoing a demand for compensation results in a positive renewal of the relationship. When a dogged insistence on just compensation results in new injustice, victims are in danger of becoming perpetrators. The only way open to an end to this cycle, is to consciously relinquish the need for just compensation. This can only be done if the injustice has been clearly identified and any legal consequences have been accepted. Whenever possible, there should be a symbolic gesture or appropriate compensation that is not too excessive. The movement of relinquishing the demand for full retribution is a movement that seems to require great sacrifice. It requires us to overcome those reactions in the soul that call out for revenge and atonement. To attain this level, we can entrust our need for justice to a higher power, whether we call it death, fate, or God.

Religious myths and images often function to resolve these difficulties. For example, the inferno of Hell is depicted according to a very precise concept of justice, or, "vengeance is mine, sayeth the Lord". But, what terrible consequences result when, possibly even in the name of our own God, we take meta-human justice into our own hands.

Family constellations often expose injustice within the family or at a societal level. A therapist must resist the temptation to stand in judgement over a family as someone who determines right and wrong and passes sentence. With great restraint, he or she listens and looks with human compassion to find what could ease the injustice and its consequences. Often, it means following one's intuition and testing out sentences that might serve as recompense. No constellation is exactly like another and no constellation can "create" justice. When all goes well, a constellation can serve as a kind of "wise resource" through the representatives' reactions and the therapist's ability to work in harmony with the forces present.

What would be the most beneficial and appropriate balance? For example, there may be a temptation in the system to blindly compensate for underlying feelings of guilt about an abortion, but such actions, even at great cost to the parents, do not help. They only serve to maintain the illusion that we can make up for something that, in reality, can never be undone or evened up. Through representatives' reactions in constellations, it seems clear that the parents' feelings of guilt and their efforts to put things right only burden the unborn child. It is as if the child, in addition to being denied life, also has to bear the responsibility for the guilt and efforts of those who are alive. What these children actually seem to want is simply to be recognised and given a place in the hearts of their parents and, occasionally, their siblings. They "rejoice" when their parents perform some small, beneficial act in memory of their denied life to demonstrate that the sacrifice was not in vain. They react best when love flows freely in the family. A humble act that does not additionally burden the aborted child, but that does something good in an appropriate measure, works quietly to resolve and bring peace.

Letting Go of Trauma

Trauma that has been buried but not resolved goes on working in relationship systems, and the symptoms often force their way back to the surface, reappearing inexplicably in the sufferer, or in someone in a later generation. Resolution lies in naming the trauma and facing it. Then, with insight, it may be possible to consciously allow the past to finish by bowing to fate and holding a loving place in the heart for those who experienced the trauma.

Sometimes, however, that is not enough. For example, if children have witnessed frightening conflicts between their parents, this experience may well be anchored in them, even if their parents later get on well together in their old age. Time does not always heal such wounds. Many constellation dynamics involve events that are long past and no longer actually happening in current relationships. The constellation, or other therapeutic intervention, then has to address the original events. The question arises how this can be done in a healing way that also avoids re-traumatisation.

The constellation process creates space for traumatic events by using representatives, but allows the client to review the events from a safe distance. The horror, pain, and terrible events are visible, but as if in a theatre performance. They may be truly horrifying, but they are not real and immediate. Still, the impact can be strong enough to have a healing effect.

Inner images arise in any case, with or without a constellation, to plague the person and re-activate the terrible experience. What is needed from a constellation or other therapeutic intervention is an effective resolution, or shift of the images, and the resolution process needs to be "retroactive". For example, a mother who was raped might be able to find peace in the arms of her own mother, or may, in some way, make peace with the rapist, perhaps in a mutual acknowledgment of their inseparable bond.

There are many effective therapeutic techniques, old and new, for treating trauma, but discussing all of them is beyond the scope of this book. In cases of systemic trauma when those involved are already dead, my personal preference in constellation work is to evoke the soul's images of "heaven", whatever they might be. Such images allow us to look at the dead in a place where we can imagine that they are at peace, instead of seeing them in the context of their traumatic experience. In this kind of image, the horror is relegated to the past. This procedure functions much as the "collapse anchor" used in NLP or other approaches.

A man was constantly angry with his mother, who had been dead for some years. During the war, when she was nine years old, she was the only member of her family to escape a bomb attack that set their house afire. She was pulled out of the house by neighbours, but watched as her parents and two younger siblings were burnt to death. This traumatic experience was, of course, deeply etched in the woman's memory. She regularly told her son about that experience, and he had to accompany her whenever possible on her almost daily trips to visit the family grave. That was much too much for any child to bear, and the boy became very angry with his mother. The therapist asked the man to close his eyes and look up into "heaven" to see his grandmother, his grandfather, and his mother's two siblings. It took some time before the man was able to look upwards and see these people. Finally he said, with his eyes still closed, "They look very friendly." When asked to imagine his mother joining her family, it again took some time for him to establish an image in his mind. Smiling, he said "This is the first time in my life that I have ever seen my mother smile." When asked how his mother looked back at him, he replied, "She isn't looking at me. She is completely happy with her family." The therapist asked, "and, when she has looked at her family long enough and then looks back at you? How will she look at you then?" In a soft, gentle voice, he answered, "With love."

Love With Clear Vision

A very simplified way of describing constellation work is, "moving from blind love to love that can see." When we are able to see the people we are blindly bound to, conscious love is free to flow. This love means: "You are you, and I am I. You have your fate and I have my fate. I remain bound to you in love forever, even if my fate is different from yours. Stay friendly if I leave you to your fate and your suffering, and go on to live my own life. I fully accept you and our family, including everything that has happened. I agree to the way everything has happened. I agree to how you are. Please stay friendly if I am the way I am. You have a place in my heart. I pass no judgements, I honour you, and I bow before what cannot be changed, for you and also for me."

We can only love when we relate to each other as separate and unique beings, as equals and of equal value. There is a deep longing in all of us to remain bound in love, even when we are different and go our own way. Love is a power that joins but also differentiates.

When a constellation works, this "love that can see" is initiated directly during the constellation work, it continues in the client's inner processes afterwards, and has concrete effects in the person's everyday life.

The Orders of Love

The philosopher and theologian Augustine once said, "Love, and do what you like." Bert Hellinger often quoted this phrase and then added, "and it is bound to be a disaster!" Our love is entwined in patterns that are not arbitrary, that we do not choose, and that cannot be changed at will. These "orders" provide a framework and love fills in the space. Love without order often ends in tragedy. Order without love remains cold and empty. A participant in one group once referred to love as "software" and order as "hardware".

There is a deep need for order in the soul. I have already mentioned the origins of the word "therapy" with its image of "coming into order". The "orders of love" play a large role in family constellations, particularly in looking at the success or failure of relationships, but are embedded in very complex and changing relationship processes. This is precisely why insight into these orders and their effects can be so helpful in difficult relationship situations.

What does order mean in this context? In a general sense, we could describe "order" as everything that follows recognisable patterns. We see repeating patterns of fate in constellations that operate, for good and for evil, in accord with the "orders" we have mentioned here, as well as others. Order can be seen as a prerequisite for the development of successful relationships. The order of conscience, for example, establishes the right place for each member of the family, hierarchy within groups, and the reliability of relationships, particularly between a man and wife and between them and their children.

Basic Orders

Within a family system, there are obvious, basic orders in terms of place and rank. Those who are there first are first and those who come later come later. In a family, the parents are there before their children. Among the children, the eldest comes first, then the second, and so on. This is an ancient order that may reflect the needs of biological survival of a group. Parents can produce offspring more quickly than children. Of the children, the eldest will be an adult sooner than younger siblings, and will soonest be in a position to care for children

79

of their own. In any case, a look at cultural history and literature reveals the importance of this ranking according to age. Jacob and Esau, the twin brothers in the Old Testament were rivals, fighting for the right to first place. Jacob, on the advice of his mother, stole this first place from his twin brother, the first-born. Presenting himself to his blind father as his brother, Esau the shepherd, he received his father's blessing and the rank of eldest, but then had to flee from his brother's wrath. Jacob later gave preference to his own youngest son, Joseph, and gave him the most beautiful clothes, with the result that Joseph's brothers wanted to kill him.

When siblings are placed in a constellation, this ancient order is reflected when they are standing next to each other, in the order of age, clockwise from their parents. In this position, children almost always feel good and at ease. This is not important in every constellation, because the focus is often on other family processes and the constellation may not even include all the siblings. When all siblings are represented, however, the therapist should pay attention to the order of ranking in any final image of resolution.

When representatives resist this hierarchy, it frequently points to unresolved dynamics in the family or some family secret in the background. For example, there were two sisters who were fighting to be in first place and the second sister always wanted to be first in her father's eyes. The conflict could not be resolved in the constellation, and later it was discovered that the first daughter was not actually the father's daughter, so the second daughter's feelings of being his "first" were justified. Sometimes siblings carry out a competitive conflict that actually belongs to their parents, or one child who pushes forward is really representing an excluded family member. Sometimes, when the line of siblings is broken and two children do not want to stand next to each other, it has turned out that there was a miscarriage or stillborn child in the gap. When a representative was added for the missing child, the siblings are able to connect again.

Competition between siblings can often be resolved very simply if parents can look at their children and say clearly, "You are my first child and you are my second child, and so on." If a mother is pregnant and inadvertently gives her three-year-old child the feeling that he or she is being replaced, that child will feel very differently about the coming event than a child who is told: "I am expecting another baby and you are going to have a little brother or sister. When you were very little I gave you lots of time and attention, and this baby will need the same. But, you will always be my first child and my biggest child."

The rank of the parents as first, before the children, also plays a role in the resolution of family conflict. If a mother's life is endangered during pregnancy and it comes to a choice between the mother's life and the child's life, the mother's life has priority, for an infant with no adult to care for it cannot survive. When extreme poverty means that everyone in the family cannot be fed, the children have to leave. In the fairy tale, Hansel and Gretel, the mother was acting in accordance with this order. This may appear monstrous to us, but the biological fact remains that small children cannot survive without adults. Fortunately, modern medicine and present-day social networks have greatly ameliorated such circumstances in much of the world. In the depths of the soul, however, the instinctual drive of archaic orders still has an effect today. It is a dynamic that also has to be taken into consideration in other groups, such as teams or companies, in order to ensure success in their common endeavours.

Constellations repeatedly show that both parents have an equal place in terms of ranking in regard to this basic order. There are other considerations of priority that will be discussed later in the context of man-woman relationships.

Orders and Complex Family Relationships

When we are dealing with two separate relationship systems, priorities stand reversed and the newer system has priority ranking over the older system. For example, when children grow up to become men and women and move into their own world of work and form their own families, the new system has priority over their families of origin. This order also serves the continuation of life. We have to leave our mother and father and "cleave to wife or husband" (in biblical language). This is a critical aspect in couples' therapy, since many marital conflicts arise out of issues connected to the two families of origin or to previous relationships. The bottom line is that loyalty to one's partner and the present family's needs takes priority over loyalty to one's parents.

The ranking of a new system over an old also affects the bonds between husband and wife. For example, if a man has married for the third time, the third marriage takes precedence over the earlier marriages. The former wives remain in their position in time and in the heart (in constellations this is again depicted in clockwise positions), but in the actual relationships, the third has priority. Otherwise, new relationships would never stand a chance. If each of these three wives has a child with this man, the basic orders and the extended orders interweave. Respecting both would mean the following order of ranking: The man has responsibility first for the child of the first marriage, then for the child of the second marriage, and then his relationship to his third wife, and finally, he and his third wife are jointly responsible for the child of the third marriage. If a woman has children from previous relationships, the same ranking operates on her side. In this way, complex family systems can usually find an order that provides the basis for successful relationships. These orders serve the care of children and allow the entire group to thrive and live in peace. Most of the time, when clients can see and understand this sense of order, they feel the sense of it immediately.

Of course, the success of any relationship is not due to these orders alone. In the same vein, if a family chooses to ignore these orders, the therapist must set aside any attitude of "knowing better", particularly if there is no true emergency. These orders have nothing at all to do with a moral stance and, in fact, are often quite opposite to the moral guidelines of a family or society. We are looking at the soul processes underlying morals and societal norms, which are geared to the continuation and care of new life.

Man and Woman

Perhaps our deepest longing is the yearning for a successful relationship, and failure to achieve such a relationship entails deep suffering. When we are looking for a resolution of conflict in couples, one possible path lies in correcting the existing imbalances in the relationship (assuming, of course, that there is love in the relationship). The fundamental order of love between partners includes a mutual exchange of taking and giving and equality in the relationship, taking individual differences into consideration. This supports the need for completion through sexuality and the continuance and care of future life. Bert Hellinger's observations on this point have elicited much criticism, but in my own experience I have found them to be very relevant and of practical value for resolving conflict in couple relationships.

The relationship between partners is nourished by a continuous flow of mutual giving and taking. One who gives has a right to receive as well, and one who takes is obligated to give in return. When one person takes more than he or she can give, over a long period of time, that partner is in debt and in a weaker position. If the debt becomes so large that it seems impossible to repay, the debtor may belittle the giver in an attempt to reduce the debt and hide the inequality. One who takes more than he or she is prepared or able to repay may have to flee from the debt by separating from that partner. In a relationship where inequality has been created by fate, for example, if one partner is unemployed or an invalid, the imbalance can be mitigated by an acknowledgement of the inequality and a sincere thank you.

One who gives more than he or she takes and persists in maintaining this imbalance stays in a superior, "better" position in an effort to avoid debt or obligation. This partner remains unreachable for the other. He or she feels under pressure because of the missing part of the exchange (taking) and frequently becomes depressed after a period of time, which of course impairs the ability to continue giving. This all-giving partner may also have to leave the relationship, but usually does so in a way that maintains his or her superiority and the right to be angry. The other partner is cast in the role of the guilty one. An individual who is incapable of taking, or unwilling to do so, will either become angry or leave. Someone who wants to give a lot in life needs a partner who is also prepared to give a lot.

A therapist who can recognise such an imbalance may be able to help the couple find a way to restore good balance, either to support their continued life together or to find a good separation. Constellations can be very helpful here because they so accurately reflect the dynamics of the couple through the representatives. The clients can step out of their usual verbal exchange and stand together as they watch from the outside. The result is a relief because exposing the patterns of repetition in their families of origin allows the couple to see their difficulties in a much larger context. It is easier to find mutually acceptable solutions when both partners can see that they are trying to free themselves from connections in a larger context, and that their conflicts do not arise merely out of malice.

The most important areas of mutual giving and taking between partners are sexuality, children (or some other mutual effort on behalf of future generations), and material provisions. Most conflicts in couple relationships arise over problems in these areas. In addition, there are all the unfulfilled expectations that partners place on one another that are actually aimed at their own parents. The partner is often called upon to fulfil needs far beyond what is actually possible. Such influences from the past skew the balance in a relationship and are usually the result of events and unresolved problems in the family of origin that have formed set attitudes and behavioural patterns. Closer to the present, disturbances to the balance of the relationship also come from the vicissitudes of fate and decisions made by the couple in the course of their relationship. There may have been an abortion or a child who was handicapped, injured by accident, or who has died. Perhaps there have been serious illnesses, unemployment, debts, children from other relationships, so-called "affairs", or other incidents.

Along with mutual giving and taking, there is a fundamental order of equality of partners in the relationship. The bond between a couple is forged in the loving act of sex, and of course a child makes the bond between the parents indissoluble. Each partner is missing something crucial that can only be supplied by the other in sexual experience.

There is a great discrepancy in what men and women have to offer towards the continuation of new life. The woman has something that a man can never equal because of her direct contact with the growing child during the pregnancy and close proximity to life and to the earth through giving birth and nursing. In addition, a woman risks her own health and her own life for the child's arrival on earth.

The man's compensating contribution is to give the mother and children protection, food, and shelter and to release the children from their tight bond to the mother. Bert Hellinger's very controversial statement that the woman follows the man (into his family, his name, his land, to his work...), and the man serves the feminine, points to this need for complementary balance.

Many external family conditions have changed in a way that make men seem less necessary. Women carry more of the burden and have more influence in the family. For example, a woman may earn her own living and there may be only one child, or perhaps no children at all. The man-woman problems sometimes increase accordingly. Contrary to the way it appears, such relationships suffer from the fact that the men lose "weight" because they no longer can, will, or need to provide for and lead their families. Both men and women suffer from the decrease in strength and useful contributions of men. From what I have observed in constellation work in many countries of the world, this is a worldwide phenomenon. It is more marked in those places where the societal and cultural contributions of men have been destroyed, for example, amongst aborigines and native peoples; or where women no longer respect men because through war, environmental destruction or "macho" attitudes, they have stopped serving future generations; or because their specific contribution seems no longer needed (as in our "advanced" countries). When men conduct themselves tyrannically and repress women and children, there is often an underlying helplessness, a need to remain in control, or a negative attempt to balance out the excess of "good" that comes from women.

Representatives in a constellation have a strong sense of balances and imbalances, what a couple are lacking, and what is needed to allow these two people to stand with equal weight facing their children. In constellations, the man usually prefers to stand to the right of the woman. This illustrates the differences between men and women and the need for each to complete oneself with the other in order to fulfil the couple relationship and the role of parents with strength. Given what has been discussed, it is not surprising that men are reluctant to stand in this position of first among equals, and they frequently need their fathers, or even a whole line of male forefathers behind them before they can take this position with strength. On the other hand, women often feel comfortable when they feel the strength and support of having a man standing to their right. In a constellation and also in real relationships, the actual determination of who occupies this place of first in service to the family is dependent upon many factors. One determining factor is if one partner has brought children from another marriage into this family, but material assets or the measure of circumstantial difficulties are also factors. In the course of a relationship there may also be changes in the situation. The therapist, who looks towards a helpful order in relationships, needs to check out the reactions of the representatives in view of the facts, and sense the "soul" weight in the dynamics of the constellation. When there is an irresolvable inequality, the therapist needs an open approach to look for alternate acceptable solutions. This might be a "thank you" or a particularly loving affection or care, or it could be some compensating effort, or perhaps separation. When those things that cannot be equalised are accepted with awareness and love, new solutions may emerge that support order in the soul. Such solutions are, of course, not arbitrary. In general, when we speak of order in constellation work, it is in the sense of a meaningful confrontation with those forces in the soul that can be brought into awareness through a constellation. The therapist must beware of communicating or imposing personal morality or standards, or even judging social developments. He or she also remains outside the everyday balance of power between the couple. The pair must develop their own insights into order and find and implement their own individual solutions, and they also have to carry the consequences themselves. The therapist can only offer experience and the constellation to show what has effects in couple relationships.

We do not exercise complete control over the consequences of our actions; our personal solutions are interwoven with societal and cultural developments that, in turn, have effects on our fate. We are formed not only by where we come from, but also by opportunities and the future that draws us forward. "What is" as well as "what might be" are influenced by multi-faceted forces of order that we cannot determine.

Giving and Taking Between Parents and Children

The relationship between parents and children depends on the fundamental order that gives parents a higher ranking, but also on another basic order. Parents give life and children take it. Whereas giving and taking between partners is reciprocal, between parents and children it is a one-way street.

Parents give life and also whatever is necessary for survival and growth. When necessary, the latter may be supplied by grandparents, foster parents, adoptive parents or even an institution. Life itself, however, comes only from parents. Simply to survive, a child must receive a great deal, and whoever receives also has to give. What a child receives is so enormous that he or she can never repay it. Life alone is so great a gift that parents can never receive adequate compensation from a child. Since receiving imposes the obligation of giving (that too is a basic law of the soul), the solution lies in the children growing up and becoming parents themselves, or taking some other appropriate action to pass life on. This is what Bert Hellinger calls "the flow of life through the generations."

The sense of debt children often feel, consciously or unconsciously, towards their parents when they leave home is also a force that moves them to develop their own lives of giving. Feelings of indebtedness usually disappear as soon as the children achieve something that holds promise for the future. Parents do, of course, receive a certain amount of recompense in the form of thanks, love, and the joy they have in their children, but that does not compare with the magnitude of the continuation of life.

When the survival of the group is at stake in times of need, everyone in a family must help everyone else. It may mean that children are also obligated to help their parents. This is the case in countries where families cannot survive if the children do not go to work. During times of war, boys sometimes have to take over the role of fathers who have been killed or are in a prisoner of war camp. A son might have to help his mother run the family farm. Adult children, of course, are also often called upon to take care of ill parents or parents who have become so old they cannot take care of themselves any longer. These kinds of help from children are a result of emergencies and last only as long as it is necessary. They must not stand in the way of the continuation of life and all that entails. Children who are forced by circumstances to sacrifice their own lives in order to take care of their parents naturally deserve recognition for that sacrifice.

When adult children take care of their elderly parents, love requires that they treat their parents with the respect due them, even if the parents become more child-like in their behaviour and demands as they grow older. A son or daughter can never really satisfy such child-like demands. It is often helpful for the caretaker child to imagine that the deceased grandparents give the elderly parents what they need to satisfy these childish demands, and children can lovingly give only what is actually needed and what is justified and appropriate.

The flow of life through the generations has an important place in constellations, and has to do with the core of health in the soul. All cultures place a high value on showing respect for ancestors who have passed life on, and a high value on the passing on of this life force.

In a seminar in the United States in which there were many Native Americans present, there was a very depressed man who wanted to do a constellation. With only a very few questions it became clear that this man's family history was extremely complicated. The therapist asked the man how many generations of ancestors he would have to have behind him in order to be strong. The Native American man considered the question and then answered, "Seven". Perhaps this was because seven is a holy number in his culture, or perhaps there was something still in order in his world seven generations earlier. In any case, representatives were chosen for seven couples and placed in a line behind this man so that he could touch the line with his back. He stood there a while, lifted his head and said in a strong, firm voice, "That feels good!" Then he looked at the therapist and said, "I have another request. Please put the seven generations in front of me that are coming after me." Seven more representatives were placed with their backs to him, facing forward in a line, one in front of the other. The man stood in the middle and beamed radiantly.

This is a beautiful image of the flow of life through the generations.

The Flow of Life: Obstacles and Solutions

There is no way to avoid taking life from one's parents. Parents cannot be any different than they are and, as far as the gift of life is concerned, it is not necessary for them to be different. Parents are parents solely because they have conceived a child and given it life; it does not depend on whether they are rich or poor, strong or weak, good or evil, warm-hearted or cold, or whether they bring up their children poorly or competently. There is great diversity, as we all know from looking at our grandparents, our parents, and ourselves. The point is to be able to take the life we have with love and a strength that looks towards the future. Many obstacles stand in the way of that kind of taking, and family constellations serve to make them visible and to resolve them whenever possible.

Children Comforting Needy Parents

Often, children look at their parents and see them as if they were needy, like children. Perhaps a grandparent died prematurely, or one of the parents was separated from their own parents for a while, or perhaps they felt disadvantaged or insufficiently cared for and supported in their own families. When children sense this childish neediness in their parents, they feel they have to respond in a way that says, in effect, "Dear Mummy/Daddy, don't be sad. I will give you what you did not get from your mother or father." The children become givers and the parents become takers.

This does not usually help in reality, but it becomes a deeply rooted pattern in the child. Although based in love, it puts the child in a presumptuous position that later causes harm. Over the course of time, a deep conflict develops in the child's soul between this desire to help and the fundamental orders that parents give and children take, that parents have a higher rank, and that children cannot intervene in their parents' fate. These conflicting movements sometimes lead to illness or depression, with the result that the individual is painfully forced back into a position of taking.

In constellations, we often see children trying to comfort one or both of their parents, making themselves big and important, as if they were the parents. When this dynamic is clear, adult clients need to help their soul-child step back from their parents and say (in some variation that suits the concrete situation): "You are big. I am small. You are my mother (father). I am the child. You give. I take."

A Partner Relationship Between Parent and Child

Similar dynamics appear when children experience their parents as needy in the context of their man-woman relationship. In this situation, children, often with the support of their parents, tend to say: "Dear Mummy (Daddy), don't be sad. I will give you what you are not getting from Daddy (Mummy)." The child becomes as big as the parent, slips into a partner role, and feels called upon to get inappropriately involved in the parents' relationship. Consider, for example, a mother who tells her 13-year-old daughter intimate details of her sexual relationship with the girl's father, or a mother who asks her 10-year-old son if she should get divorced or not; or a father who goes on holiday with only his daughter, or demands that his son take his side in a marital conflict. Sexual abuse is an especially grave case of blurred boundaries between parents and children.

Children blithely jump into gaps that are left in their parents' feelings. Sometimes they are encouraged, or even forced, to stand in for one parent in relationship to the other. The consequences here can be serious. Again, we see the inner, usually unconscious, conflict between a presumptive attitude, assumed with love because of necessity or demand, and the archaic prohibitions against confusing the boundaries between children and parents. Many of the Greek tragedies are examples of such confusions. In serious cases, consequences may lead to a battle between father and son or between mother and daughter with the unspoken message: "It is you or me; only one of us can occupy this place with Mother (Father)." In extreme cases this dynamic has even led to murder, but even in less dramatic cases, later relationships are often burdened and the individuals concerned are plagued by feelings of guilt. Sometimes the children of such families choose not to have any children of their own or, if they do, they repeat the same pattern with their own partner and children.

The dynamics show up in constellations when a son stands next to his mother, in the place where her husband should be, or when a daughter is standing by her father as if she were his wife. Sometimes they can stand in this position very naturally and at ease, but most of the time the children feel very burdened and want to move away from the parent. The therapist can help the adult child to extradite himself or herself from the entanglement with a parent's needs by articulating something appropriate to the situation that clearly states the connections between the client's issue and this entanglement in the parents' relationship. It could be a sentence such as, "Please Mum (Dad), stay friendly if I pull away. I love you and I love Dad (Mum). Let me out from under the burden of your relationship. I am only your daughter (son)."

Interrupted Reaching-Out Movements and a Refusal to Reach Out

If a child is separated from his or her parents, particularly the mother, at an age when the child cannot understand the separation, there is an interruption in the loving reaching-out movement towards the mother, and sometimes also towards the father. This is particularly prevalent if the child's life was endangered. The younger the child, the more important it is to have close body contact with the mother. The reaching-out movement is obviously interrupted if one parent dies prematurely, if a child is given away to someone else, if the child remains in hospital after birth for some necessary medical intervention and the mother is unable to stay with her child or cannot stay close enough, or if the mother is in hospital and the little one is cared for by someone else. A very young child cannot understand such a separation and feels abandoned, helpless, and cut off from all familiar warmth and security. A child's reaction is often a refusal to take the mother back in, even if the separation ends well. You can observe this phenomenon in children who are picked up by their mother when it is time to leave the hospital. They may kick and scream and throw their head back, or they may remain absolutely apathetic, with dulled eyes, and no look of joy for their mother. Sometimes a mother cannot hold out against the child's will when she feels herself being shut out. She does not trust herself to hold the child firmly in her arms until trust is re-established and love can flow again. The rift between the mother and child deepens and remains, even though life in the family may seem to return to normal.

A man in a group referred to his mother as murder-mother, but there was no mother in his family system who was actually a murderer. The story that came out was this: When the man was just barely two years old, he and his mother were bombed out in Berlin and had to find refuge in a small cabin in the country. The boy's father was away at war and no relatives lived nearby, so the mother had to try to get by with her son in this cabin, about half an hour away from the nearest village. One day the boy became seriously ill with a high fever and his mother had to fetch the doctor. She left him alone in the cabin and ran the long way to the village. From there she rang the doctor in the nearest city. By the time he got to the village and they ran back to the cabin, the boy had been alone for a long time. When the doctor finally got to the child and looked at him, he pronounced the boy dead. He was not dead, however, and they nursed him back to life.

In view of this history, we can perhaps understand where the word "murder-mother" belongs. The therapist had the client stand for himself as a young child, but when the therapist, representing his mother, wanted to take him in her arms and hold him, he broke out in a cold sweat. With repeated reassurance from the therapist that things had actually turned out all right, he could slowly let go of his panic. He allowed the woman to take him in her arms and wept in despair. All of his anxiety, created by the nearness of death, burst out, but this time in the protective arms of the therapist standing in for his mother.

Such processes point to personal trauma that may have no direct systemic background in and of themselves, but sometimes appear in a systemic connection that magnifies the trauma, for example, if the mother had also had a near-death experience as a child, or if she had been unable to cope with her situation as a single parent.

An interrupted reaching-out movement towards a parent shows its effects primarily in later relationships and the person's experience of closeness and distance. For example, when a man who was separated from his mother in childhood falls in love with a woman who wants close contact with him, who wants to love him and be loved by him, he may reflexively shy away from this intimacy, as if something in him refuses to trust again and risk being abandoned once again. He may prefer to pull away himself to avoid the risk. All the feelings of that small child come up again: his fear and perhaps anger, his feelings of helplessness, his resignation, and his withdrawal. Closing off the loving reaching-out movement to a mother leads to an interruption of the flow of love between a couple, and sometimes to their children as well. It also leads to a general mistrust of anyone who gets close, and to life itself.

When there seems to be no systemic basis to explain a reluctance to take parents or the failure of a relationship, we often find a traumatic separation experience somewhere in the background. A group constellation is much too brief to fully resolve an interrupted reaching-out movement. Difficulties of this nature and other issues related to personal trauma require a more specific therapeutic support.

A refusal to reach out is usually connected to systemic issues, coupled with personal traumatic experiences. When a child is treated badly by his or her parents, abused or deeply hurt, or excluded, an interrupted reaching-out movement often later manifests as a refusal to reach out. The child, and later the adult, closes off his or her heart and hardens against the parent. This closing movement is what has consequences for later relationships, for one's attitude towards life, and perhaps also for health. Sometimes parents are not even aware of the effects of their words and behaviour on their children, and certainly did not intend to set this chain reaction in motion. They cannot sense how incidents in the family history are connected to their actions and have led to their children's refusal to reach out. What happens to a rebellious little boy, for example, when his brother, his mother's "sunshine", dies and his mother, in the throes of grief and helpless rage says: "I wish you had died instead of him?"

Resolution is difficult to find in these cases, and can usually be found only if the adult child is able look at his or her parents and bow deeply before their fate. The parents may also need to bow before their fate in order to bring themselves and their child back into the flow of love.

Blame

Blaming also hampers love between children and their parents and prevents children from moving into the future with strength and success. Strangely enough, people who blame their parents often live their lives with a very meagre exchange of giving and taking, even though they may have received a great deal from their parents. Blaming parents seems to be a privilege enjoyed only by children in rich countries.

Anyone who has received a lot also feels a pressure to give generously. For those who find this burden too difficult or unacceptable in some way, the only option is to belittle or disparage what has been received in order to reduce the obligation to make compensation.

Here, we also need to ask the question that runs through all constellation work: "What lies behind this blaming? Where are the deeper bonds and the deeper love?" If we expand our vision to a larger systemic context, we often find other people in the system whose suffering has contributed to the parents' well being. It turns out very often to be the case that a child who feels critical of his or her parents is looking, consciously or unconsciously, at those who have paid a high price. In consideration of them, the child finds it difficult to take from these parents with a clear conscience. The protest generation of the late sixties, with all their criticism and blaming of society, may have been responding to the Holocaust, the victims of war, the forced labour workers, and the poverty in developing countries. They looked at evil in the world and had doubts about the right to bring children into such a world, or their right to live such a protected life of luxury. They despised their parents who showed little empathy for the victims and countered by saying to the previous generation, "You want the best of us, but you won't get it."

> There was a man who had inherited a number of bakeries, but sold them and lost all the money in questionable financial investments. He became ill and ended up living on social assistance. He accused his now-deceased parents of having spent all their time and energy on the family business, and of having given him money but never love. As he examined his family history more carefully, he discovered more of the truth. The actual history was that his grandfather had built the bakery chain on the basis of many Jewish businesses, acquired when Jewish families had to sell out cheaply in order to flee the country. The Jewish descendents later made demands for compensation, but they were rejected.

Those victims, however, were not helped at all by this client's blaming refusal to take, nor by his reluctance to give. The constellation helped the client to find a way to take what was good from his parents, despite the fact that someone else had paid the price for it. He had to see and honour the victims to give meaning to their suffering and the price they had paid. Providing something good for those in the future can compensate for the sacrifices that have been made and can open a path for the living persons to continue on and do something positive in their lives.

Depression

Depressed people cannot take from their parents, but are prepared to give a lot in their lives. One could call depression a disease of the roots. It is as though the person is cut off from his or her roots (parents), and the sap of life cannot be sucked in, so the plant dries up. Anyone who gives but does not take will become empty and hollow inside after a time, and may fall into a serious depression. Then, giving is impossible and the illness finally may force the person to accept help from others.

When people have difficulty taking from their parents and, consequently, taking from others later in life, it is again appropriate to ask what deeper forces of love are at work in the background? Sometimes even a very young child's experience of his or her parents is that they seem overwhelmed or perhaps in mortal danger. Something in the child's soul holds back from making any additional demands on such parents, for fear of overloading them. A child lives in dread of a parent collapsing or dying because the child has taken too much. The child attempts to protect his or her parents by remaining separate and independent. If this develops into a fundamental pattern, the child becomes depleted and must live with all the consequences of that.

What is the solution? It is usually not enough to look only at the relationship between parents and children; the grandparents are also involved. What is needed is for the parents' souls to connect to their own parents in such a way that they can get what they lack and no longer feel overwhelmed and endangered. We need to look for the specific events in the past that interrupted the flow through the generations. That is where the healing can begin.

> In a group there was a very depressed woman who had been hospitalised many times in a clinic for psychosomatic illness. She was hoping to find a way to improve her relationship with her mother. When asked to set up a constellation of herself and her mother, she placed the two facing each other, but at a great distance, and the atmosphere was ice cold. With no further information, the therapist added another woman to represent the client's grandmother. Nothing happened and the atmosphere remained frigid. Another woman was added for the great-grandmother. Then the grandmother spontaneously moved to the great-grandmother and threw

herself in her arms, weeping bitterly. After a while, she approached her own daughter, the client's mother, and held her lovingly. Beaming, she finally went to the client's representative, the youngest link in the chain, and embraced her warmly.

The client, who was watching from the group, took a deep breath and asked permission to join the women. All four embraced for a long time. The client had no idea what had happened between her grandmother and her great-grandmother, but she obviously felt greatly relieved. That evening she had a long telephone conversation with her mother and discovered the story. Her great-grandmother had been an unwed mother and at the insistence of her parents she had sent her newborn to distant relatives in a faraway city. Later, they refused to give the child (the grandmother) back to her mother.

Usually, when children are worried that their parents cannot bear any additional burden, it is because there have been deaths or other painful, terrible events that in some way have pushed these parents to the limit or to the precipice of their own death.

Spirituality

There are some forms of spirituality, religiosity, or meditative practices that cut adult children off from their parents and ancestors, and that constrict the flow of life.

This is the most "elegant" way to refuse to take from one's parents. It is not so self-destructive and also contains a grain of good. The argument is, essentially, that parents do not really give life; life is much greater than something parents could "make", and comes from somewhere beyond. When people do not wish to thank their parents, for whatever reason, it is very appealing to divert round them and go directly to the greater power, declare that they take life, and gladly give thanks. Taking from a greater power but excluding one's parents and ancestors usually results in a lack of life energy, strength, and a lively exchange of giving and taking.

For example, a young father who went off to India for a year to meditate was not at all concerned about his small son left at home. There are particular communities where one is invited to get closer to God by leaving one's parents and family. Some people become strict vegetarians to avoid feeling any guilt towards animals. When we look at what lies behind such spiritual movements, it is often the case that parents or ancestors were burdened by guilt of some kind. Their child fears that if he or she takes from the parents, the guilt or debt will have to be taken on as well. Avoiding close contact with these parents and family is one way round the problem.

There is nothing more frightening, from the "spiritual" person's point of view, than to be guilty. For example, "make love, not war" is a slogan that indicates a fear of guilt, but does not necessarily point to a responsible way to handle love. Some people fall into a kind of spiritual "compulsion" and constrict their everyday life to a great degree. Others seek out a place far from home, perhaps secure in a spiritual community, as if geographical distance could protect one from participating in guilt. Sometimes this actually seems like the only route to survival.

A constellation can help to clarify guilt connections in the family and help people take life from a greater power, but concretely through their parents and ancestors, including the guilt and all its consequences. Everyone who lives is guilty in some form. What is most beneficial in the world is treating one's own guilt, and that of others, in a responsible way and in a way that clears the path for the future. The forms of spirituality and religiosity that remain firmly grounded in this way develop life-affirming, constructive and empathetic strength.

Please, Thank You, Yes, and Yes to Adversity

Sometimes, what happens in constellation groups seems like a kind of "soul" work or something religious. And perhaps the positive reception the work has enjoyed is an indication of a basic need for fulfilment that is not given enough importance in modern society. The constellation opens a space that allows people to reach-out in love to their parents without excluding evil, failure and guilt. Group participants draw close to each other and establish a warm feeling of togetherness. To say "please", "thank you", and "yes" to reality as it is, is a very simple act of completion in the soul, but often one that is very difficult to achieve. It may sound easy to find the kind of love in our lives that does not exclude anyone or anything, but it is actually a major achievement and a great gift. Agreeing to a life filled with love is something that feels good and it has a powerful impact. It is a movement that allows us to entrust ourselves to the "flow of life" and to enter more fully into our lives with all our abilities and opportunities. It is also necessary to say "yes" to adversity. The power of saying "yes" to life lies in speaking this word even in the face of failure or negative experiences. It is always possible that failure, injustice, and pain may lead on to something positive, but in and of itself, they remain hurtful to us or to others. If the final outcome of our adversity is suffered without having authentically spoken "yes", we perish. If it is not conscious and acknowledged with awareness, our "yes" loses its grounding and its power to change. We can say "yes" when the negative aspects are integrated into a larger context. The following story "*The Row*" may clarify how "yes" and "no" can connect in our lives:

> There were two women who had been engaged in an on-going row. One of them was a "yes" person and the other was "nay-sayer". Whereas the one could always be counted on to nod her head yes, the other always shook her head no. Consequently, they could never get together on anything. Because they cared for each other, however, they went to a wise teacher and asked for advice. The teacher asked each of them to put forth her views. The yea-sayer said, "We can only be in harmony with life when we say yes to life." The nay-sayer said, "We can only contribute to a life that is better if we reject the way life is now."
>
> The teacher said, "A person's head is very mobile. It can nod, it can shake, and it can even turn in circles. I will give you a three-fold answer. The first answer is: Never say a yes that is really a no and never say a no that is really a yes. The second answer is: Whatever opposes you in your daily life, take it as an opportunity to accept life and move forward in your learning. When you have taken everything in this way, then say no to anything that keeps you from respecting, loving, and acting. The third answer is: One who differentiates understands; one who brings differences together grows; and one who has trust in an integrating force is secure.
>
> The women felt satisfied with this answer and as they walked away, arm-in-arm, they moved their heads in time to their steps.

Therapy, in the broadest sense of the word, can only succeed when both therapist and client are willing to perceive and accept reality as it is, with all its complexity, with all its binding and resolving dynamics, and with all its constraints and supports. Still, it must be sufficiently differentiated in terms of the realities of each individual family system. This multiplicity and simplicity is what supports health in the soul. We can only grow through interaction with what actually is, which demands that a constellation leader's systemic knowledge and interventions be appropriately individualised.

4 Elements of Constellation Work – More Than Merely a Method

Family constellations can be described as a professionally guided method for dealing with personal and family crises. As such, it is a method that can be taught and that can be learned. Both the teaching and the learning require a high degree of openness to the subtleties of the method. We tend to expect the same kind of problem-solving methods in psychological areas that we find in the natural sciences and technical areas, offering dependability, and predictability. We want methods that are guaranteed and that offer certainty and, if possible, predictability and beneficial results.

Psychotherapy, counselling, and the care of the soul, however, are very personal processes. The workings of the soul are so individual and complex that there are no appropriate technical approaches. We can, of course, set general goals for a process of healing and change; for example, we could say that people normally do better when they are at peace with their parents and live in supportive relationships. We do not know in advance, however, how this goal might look concretely for any one individual, nor how it might be achieved with that person.

In any method there is a temptation to pay more attention to technique than is actually useful and meaningful.

In the realm of the soul, however, individual and social meaning is of primary importance, and methods are less important than end results. It is similar to a technical approach to painting, playing a musical instrument, or writing poetry. There is a certain degree of technique required that can be learned and practised, but technique will not allow us to predict, control, or guarantee what is going to come out in the picture, the music, or the poem. In addition, the "score" of a family constellation can only be played once.

The following discussion of the procedures of family constellations is not meant as a tool for learning techniques, but rather to aid understanding of the processes significant to constellation work. Many people say that the end justifies the means, but we could also say, the means reveal the end. From this point of view, it is clear how the individual elements of family constellation procedures serve the overall process of improving relationships.

Constellation work is defined as a phenomenological approach, which means remaining as free as possible from preconception and judgement. It means facing the reality that emerges in a constellation with openness and without aims. In a certain sense, the phenomeno-logical method is a paradox because openness implies reaching out towards something to take it in. Only one who is trying to see and to move can be free of intention. The practice of not knowing is only a virtue for a person of knowledge. Therefore, attempting to utilise a phenomenological method in constellations requires a dual track approach: knowing and not knowing, intention and lack of intention, openness and taking in, direct awareness of reality (phaenomeno-) and interpretation of meaning in the mind (logie).

Certain Zen stories describe an openness to phenomena that is similar to the attitude in family constellations.

> Tchou-tchou asked his master Nan Chuan, "What is the true path?"
> Nan Chuan answered, "The everyday path is the true path."
> Tchou-tchou asked, "Can one learn this path?"
> Nan Chuan replied, "The more you learn, the further you get from the path."
> Then Tschou-tchou asked, "If one cannot find the path through learn-ing, how does one recognise it?"
> Nan Chuan said, "The path is not a visible thing and it is not an invisible thing. It is not recognisable, and also not unrecognisable. Do not seek it, do not learn it, and do not name it! Be as open and as wide as the sky and you will be on the path!"

Contact

In a group setting, a family constellation usually begins with a client coming to sit next to the therapist. Sometimes, the group leader may begin the group with an introductory round, whereby participants in-troduce themselves and state briefly what their issue is. If so, the first contact occurs in this exchange, sometimes including input from the therapist clarifying an issue, sometimes providing the impetus for a participant to begin looking inwards, sometimes including reports of impressions or personal stories that open the horizons of the group and each of the individual participants.

The actual step leading to a constellation, however, begins with the physical proximity of the client to the therapist. It is a significant step for someone to leave his or her place among the other participants and approach the therapist in full view of everybody in the group. This movement provides initial information about the readiness and energy of this particular client to seek resolution through a constellation. The movement of the client towards the therapist draws the attention of everyone in the group as well as that of the therapist, and focuses attention on what is about to happen. This establishes the "field" that enables and carries the whole constellation. The therapist and the group tune in to the soul field of the client, a field that each person carries, in the way a radio can be tuned to the wavelength of a particular radio station. This kind of attention is required to ensure that whatever happens actually has something to do with this client and his or her family, and not just a "jumble of wavelengths" or something coming from an altogether different transmitter. Attention and respect are needed to open, carry, and complete a constellation.

Sometimes a participant asks to work, but is actually only volunteering because no one else has stepped forward and this person feels a need to fill the gap. Sometimes a client might make comments that divert attention in a different direction, or diffuse the focus of the work, for example, expressing anxiety about doing a constellation or commenting on the pressure he or she feels, or a desire to get it over with. Comments like these focus the energetic attention on a momentary feeling or a temporary intention. They narrow the focus of attention to those feelings and behaviour that are most familiar and typical for this person. This constriction will most likely hamper movement towards the client's real distress and any relevance to this family.

The therapist might interpret this as a signal that the time is not yet optimal for successful constellation work with this person. Sometimes, however, the therapist can appropriately guide the client towards a more centred approach to the process, so that the distracting feelings and comments make way for a quiet, strong sense that the self is open to something new and essential.

A curious experience is that some constellations are awaited with bated breath from the very first moment by the therapist and the entire group. In other situations, the client's movement towards the therapist attracts little attention and there is a feeling of restlessness in the group. Sometimes, this may be attributable to a previous constellation that was unsettling or dissatisfying in some way, or to a precipitous shift from one constellation to the next. In the main, though, an individual seems to send out a wordless message to the group that either focuses their full attention on this fate and what is about to happen, or one that does not capture the group's full attention.

Once the client is seated next to the therapist, they first make contact silently. If the clients begin to speak immediately about their state at the moment or in general, the therapist may ask them to sit for a moment, breathe deeply, perhaps close their eyes, and put their trust in the resolution that is not yet visible and in the process of the coming constellation of their family. This quiet period at the beginning can be very brief, or it might last several minutes, but it serves to bring clients into harmony with themselves and their families. Wordlessly, the person makes contact with his or her own life, relationship fields, the present issue, and the future, without any attempt to direct the process. The therapist tunes into this client and the person's family, but also into the larger field that holds this family. The therapist, too, has to avoid thinking about what might emerge, and must simply open up to the client in a friendly way and be ready to feel and sense the forces in the soul field of this client that might lead to resolution.

In this harmonising process, the therapist receives a sensory impression from the client's face. Perhaps this face is drawn and tight, perhaps in reverie, or the face of an elderly woman might reflect a quality of a young child, or vice versa, the face of a young man may look very much like his great-grandfather, and one can imagine a stiff handlebar moustache from a past era. Some people look down their noses, others look dark and foreboding, and yet others gaze at the floor in a depressed way. This could be an opportunity for a small, initial therapeutic intervention, such as guiding a stiffly erect head to assume a bowed position of humility. A brief but accurate therapeutic observation can help the person get in touch with important sensory information or feelings, thereby sidestepping more routine patterns of awareness. Quite often even such minimal interventions allow pain to surface and clients often begin to weep or to breathe more deeply and calmly.

The differences between people become visible in this first phase of the process, even before the issue has been broached. Not every client feels heavily burdened as they approach the therapist. Sometimes, there is a cheerful, light exchange and tension-relieving laughter. Other times, the therapist and client may proceed directly to the issue at hand.

It is important to allow the necessary degree of focus, strength and tension to develop in all these initial contacts between a client and the therapist, between the client and the group, and between this client and his or her presenting issue, life situation, relationships and fate.

Family constellation work is a systemic method. This means that from the first contact with this client, the therapist is concerned with the matrix of the client's family system and identity groups, and the client is understood in the context of his or her "soul field", which extends beyond the boundaries of the individual person. The therapist is responsive to the client, but also to that person's parents and the bonds of love in the person's culture or community. During the entire constellation process, the therapist looks at problems and solutions that involve the whole family system. Although clients are usually looking for a personal solution to a personal problem, the therapist operates on the assumption that such a solution will develop out of a resolution of the unresolved and unfinished issues in the system as a whole.

Therefore, although the therapist may be aware of a subliminal invitation to enter into a personal relationship with the client, it is understood that this invitation is unconsciously meant for the client's parents and the therapist remains abstinent. Clients, or observers watching from the outside sometimes experience this stance as cold or unfeeling. The therapist, however, must remain unwaveringly friendly towards the entire family system. Reducing problems and solutions to the viewpoint of one individual is already part of the problem. If we seriously consider what influences us in life, what we experience and learn, what we hope for and want, and what we decide, it is impossible to avoid the fact that we are bound to our primary caretakers and often further, to larger social forces or vicissitudes of fate.

Even our personal traumatic experiences are still connected to a larger context. Personal trauma often requires a specific kind of individual therapy, and not all injury arises from a shared fate; in terms of effects and coping mechanisms, however, individual trauma is also connected to conscious and unconscious relationship fields.

At the same time, there is no relationship system that exists independently of the individuals within it. There are no personal relationships without the people involved. The therapist must remain aware of the client as an individual person, but always in the context of identity groups, to a greater or lesser degree.

The Issue

Family constellations are most effective in response to an urgent need and a serious issue. These are the factors that provide strength and focus in the field and that guide the client, therapist, and representatives through the constellation. When the problem or issue can be clearly formulated by the client, it helps the work to flow more easily.

A problem that is open to solution is usually one that can be expressed in one sentence and understood immediately by everyone. It can be formulated openly, without explanations of causes or conditions for solutions. Issues that are orientated towards the future are more useful than a desire for understanding things in the past. An issue supported by facts is more useful than just feelings in opening a path that leads with ease and energy towards real help. Interestingly, clients with such clear issues can articulate them while looking directly at the therapist, whereas looking at the floor often leads to a confused description and vague feelings.

Some examples of clear concerns are: "I have suffered from depression for years," "my mother committed suicide last year," "I want to leave my wife but I can't do it," "our son is hyperactive and we are very worried," "I have been at odds with my sister ever since our parents died," "I have cancer." But, of course, it is not always possible for someone to formulate a problem clearly, and the true weight in the soul is not always signposted by touching emotions, clear symptoms, or a significant family fate. Sometimes, a course participant might simply say that he has come because his wife asked him to. Or there may be vague wishes such as: "I want to be freer", "I want to grow up", "I want to find myself and be more self-confident." If issues like these do not come from a personal desire or a yearning for self-discovery, they are not strong enough for a constellation. Such issues will not strike resonance in the collected, focussed attention of the group.

There are constellation leaders who refuse to work with such issues and prefer to wait for the client to come to a clear formulation of an issue that lends itself to a constellation. One can, however, look for the real issues lying beneath the surface, and assist the client with this clarification. If the therapist has a feeling that there is enough energy present, despite a vague formulation, this may indicate something of importance in the family background. For example, if the client is complaining about not being able to find his or her place in life, we need to understand what this means. The therapist might ask if the person grew up with his or her own parents. Perhaps the answer is "yes"; the therapist then asks if the person is married and has children, and the answer is again "yes". The therapist asks if the client has a job, and if things are going well in that regard. The client is, indeed, employed and reports that things are more or less satisfactory in this area. Then, we may suspect that the distress lies in the system and the question might be, "Who was it that actually had no place in life?"

It is astounding how often it then becomes clear where the problem actually belongs. Perhaps there was an illegitimate child of the father's, where contact was broken off, or the mother had a child that was put up for adoption, or some similar situation. A wish for freedom in one's life often reveals a hidden desire to die, since only death can grant absolute freedom. If the therapist asks the provocative question, "Do you want to die?" the answer is often "Yes", but sometimes a vehement, "No!" In either case, the formulation generally takes on weight and shape.

Vaguely formulated but highly charged issues often have an underlying structure that becomes clear if we take the formulation literally. If someone says he or she is longing to be free, the therapist might ask who in the system was locked up? If a person expresses a desire to be more adult, the logical question to ask is who died prematurely and was therefore denied a chance to become an adult? Someone who is engaged in a search for self might be unconsciously expressing the fate of an aunt who mysteriously disappeared, or a grandfather who went missing in action during the war. Behind many issues that seem to belong to the repertoire of self-development but actually lead in circles, there are often real events in the history of the family. When these stories are told, they provide energy for a constellation and resolution.

If it is not possible to define the issue in the course of a brief dialogue in such a way that the client, the therapist, and the group become curious about the constellation, the therapist will have to interrupt the work until a later time. The main reason constellations fail is that they are begun even when there is a feeling that the problem, as it is stated, cannot carry the work.

It is not only vagueness of formulation that prevents a constellation from flowing. The chances of a successful constellation are also diminished when the client is closed or narrowly fixated on his or her predicament, without a sense of openness to others in the family and their fates, or if the client remains cold and dismissive, or if the person is too attached to the problem or to his or her own solutions.

Is there a "right" moment to do a constellation? We do not really know, but the therapist has to make the decision based on contact with the client, the thrust of the issue, and the way it is formulated. If the therapist feels supported by the client's "soul field", then the next step of the constellation can be taken; if not, the process is interrupted until such time as there is enough energy available. There has to be sufficient energetic tension in the issue and the client's need to capture the attention and focus of the therapist and the group, and the therapist also needs to have a clear sense that this client is capable of carrying on the process that will be set in motion by a constellation. Sometimes, the therapist feels weighed down, and feels that he or she has to supply the missing energy and do the client's work. Some clients seem to have too little energy and others are too impatient to "let" things emerge, and want to take matters energetically into their own hands.

In answer to the question of when is the right moment, I sometimes tell the following story:

> In one of his many attempts to research stimulus-response mechanisms, Pavlov tested a dog's behaviour in the following way: A chain link fence was set up, with fresh meat on one side. A dog was led into the other side. In the first trial, the dog was brought to the test area in a normal state of hunger. The dog ran the length of the fence round to the other side, and devoured the meat. In a second trial, the dog was brought in after having been fed to a point of satiation. Predictably, the dog was not interested in the meat on the other side of the fence, and lay down and went to sleep. A third time, the dog was brought in after several days of insufficient food. The dog caught the scent of the meat, rushed the fence, and tried to bite his way through. He got so caught in the fence that it was difficult to extricate him.

Therefore, the best moment for a constellation is when someone is in a "normal state of hunger".

The way a client expresses a readiness to do a constellation and the way an issue is formulated also depend upon the attitude of the therapist. If a therapist asks concise questions about the issue, need, or desire, it usually encourages a concise answer. A therapist's courage and capacity to face whatever fate is revealed will encourage trust and openness on the part of the client. A therapist's skill in differentiating between what is essential and what is irrelevant, and in determining the importance of an issue for the soul can help point the client towards core issues. A therapist who is friendly and unbiased towards everyone in the family and towards everything that has happened makes it easier for clients to open up in a loving and respectful way to the others in their family and their lives, but also to themselves.

Watching a constellation for the first time, one could easily get the impression that the issue itself plays only a minor role. Constellations develop in directions that often appear to have little or nothing to do with the original issue. Actually, information from the client about family events or the spontaneous movement of representatives often do shift the focus of the constellation. In general, it works best if neither the therapist nor the client gets fixated on the problem or symptoms and solutions. Any fixed idea that there has to be a resolution is already a constraint to the healing process in the soul.

The basic question that has proven most productive for guiding a constellation is, "What is the soul trying to bring into order?" or "How is the soul seeking harmony and peace?" This kind of open question allows resolution to appear in a surprising way, perhaps in some area that we would not necessarily expect, given the nature of the original issue. Sometimes, the best answer appears when the question has receded into the background. Still, the original issue and its connections to the family soul are what provide energy for the constellation. The most satisfying resolution is one in which the systemic connections also provide an "aha!" experience in terms of the presenting problem or question.

Information

A constellation requires very little concrete data. In fact, it is essential that information be limited to only what is absolutely necessary. A constellation is always a unique event, even if the same client does more than one constellation, or if a constellation is done as part of on-going therapy or counselling. The limited time available in one constellation only allows for a limited amount of information. Otherwise, the process becomes too diffuse and the result is confusion.

A good way to assess and limit the data is to look at its strength and energy, and whether the therapist and group are energised by the information or if the interest level drops. Further indicators of significance are: relevance to the presenting problem, the impact of the information on the listener, internal images that spontaneously emerge, and, of course, the objective weight. A suicide in a family always carries a significant weight, even if the constellation progresses in a different direction or if the client considers it unimportant (which is often, in itself, a sign that the opposite is true).

We are concerned here with objective events and the fate of family members, not with how these were subjectively experienced. Sometimes, however, a brief recounting of personal experience might point to an important family event. We are not considering the characteristics of family members, even if that would seem to provide information about relationships between individuals. It is usually unimportant what someone looks like or how they act, when what we are primarily interested in is the fact that this person is a mother or a father, or perhaps died prematurely. If a client comments, "My father was a very weak man," it may be an indication of that father being devalued and, as such, is noted by the therapist and may provoke an intervention, but usually diverts attention away from the father and his fate. The more relevant information probably concerns the father and his own family, which may cast a different light on his "weakness", and open the way to a new relationship between the father and his son.

Personal characterisation is not desirable if both client and therapist are to keep their attention on what is essential. However it has to be handled in a way that does not negatively influence the therapist's rapport with the client, but rather deepens it.

> In answer to the therapist's question about significant events in his family, a man responded with a comment about his father's weakness. He said that well into his seventies, his father had held on to a small business despite always hovering on the brink of bankruptcy. The therapist commented, "Hats off to your father for having kept a failing company afloat for so long to support his family." This comment brought a light into the man's eyes. It was clear that in his heart he felt supportive of his father. The important factor was the therapist's reframing, which left the client free to look at the real burden of fate in his family. His mother's father had committed suicide after having lost everything in a currency reform after the war. In the constellation, the phrase "weak father" turned out to belong to the client's mother, and referred to her own father and his actions.

What information is needed for a family constellation? Basically, what is of importance is whatever informs the processes of loving bonds as described in the previous chapter. The first question has to do with the client's family: father, mother, siblings, grandparents, aunts and uncles, previous partners of parents or grandparents, half-siblings of the client or parents, and perhaps people from earlier generations if there were significant circumstances. Some non-family members also belong to the system if the family owes them something in an essential way (for example, foster parents, adoptive parents, a childless neighbour or friend who has passed on material possessions to this family). If a member of the family has caused injury to another, intentionally or not, or is indebted to someone, that person belongs to the family system. When the situation is reversed and an injury or debt has been inflicted by someone else, this person is also included in the family system. The dead are included, as far back as the memories of living family members reach. Belonging that is due to a turn of fate sometimes extends even further back. In some constellations, a long-deceased ancestor is added even though no current information is available about this person. Usually, however, the therapist limits the persons involved to those who are reachable through the information available.

In addition to the question of who belongs to the system, the other important enquiry is about what has actually happened. Significant events in families include stillbirths, miscarriages, life-threatening births, abortions, disruption of living space (for example through immigration or exile), separation of children from one or both parents, separation of parents, unknown paternity, painful loss of people or possessions, all premature deaths, family feuds, long periods of unemployment or disability, serious illnesses, addictions, accidents, war-related experiences, injustices, suicides, psychiatric hospitalisation, and any other major events.

A statement of resolution is characterised by its focus on the fate of all family members. This may seem unfamiliar to some people, since in psychotherapy and counselling we are accustomed to looking at problems, including their origins and their reciprocal effects within the system, only in terms of the client's experience and the client's immediate surroundings. The client's experiences are important in family constellations, particularly when they are of a traumatic nature, but they are considered within a context that is larger than what is usual in our everyday thinking. When we are confronted by social behaviour that is conspicuous, disturbing, or dangerous in some way, we tend to interpret it according to what we experienced in our childhood, how our parents behaved, and how we were raised. We look through the lens of what we were encouraged or forced to learn, and required to do, or to tolerate. We imagine emotional effects as a result of immediate, linear or reciprocal influences. To be sure, we sometimes include information about previous generations, but our focus is usually on direct interaction.

Family constellations, on the other hand, look at people in the context of their entire family history, including connections that lie outside what is directly communicated. Many feelings and actions that are problematic for us and for others cannot be comprehended in terms of direct experience. Much of what is offered as an explanation for the behaviour of parents and children or, in a larger context, for individuals and society, is simply not sufficient to solve the problems. One major reason many people are attracted to family constellation work is that exploring their own experiences and drawing conclusions about their problems based on that information has not proven helpful. Information that the client is missing is also of importance. The sources of many problems lie hidden behind unknown events and destinies in a family.

On the other hand, the wider perspective of a family constellation does not invalidate a narrower perspective of personal experience. Sometimes, family constellations run the risk of seeking solutions at the level of destiny and offering interpretations that do not resolve, or that are incomprehensible, because they do not adequately take into account the client's personal experience, which may be pivotal in this particular context.

In looking for information that will carry a constellation forward, it is useful to distinguish between information and impressions that are likely to lead to personal trauma (such as an early, traumatic separation from the mother), and events and awareness that point towards systemic connections (for example, the client's mother's traumatic separation from her mother as they were fleeing their homeland). Of course, both kinds of events may be present and interconnected in their present effects on the individual. Actual facts, the style of presentation, and the general impression the client makes all combine with the therapist's feelings, intuitions, resonance with the client, insight, and experience to indicate the depth of work that may be realistically attainable.

It makes little sense and is, in any case, hardly possible to collect all potentially relevant information before starting a constellation.

That would result in a boring process that is more likely to hinder and confuse than to provide a clear orientation for the constellation. The therapist and the client both need access to the information that is essential, hopefully without major diversions. If a client has first experienced constellations of others in the group, it is easier to identify the significant events in his or her own family history. The critical factors in determining what information will be helpful are: the therapist's intuition, awareness of the client's behaviour and appearance, an openness to being guided towards hypotheses by the client's problem itself, and an assessment of the weight of various aspects.

The therapist's initial "intuition" deepens and eases the development of the constellation when it touches on what is essential. There will be a resonance in the attentiveness of the group and clear, sometimes surprising reactions from the client. For example, if the therapist detects a subliminal, "strange" anger, he or she can ask the client directly, "Which member of your family does your anger belong to?" The client might answer very matter-of-factly, "My father". Or, the answer may be a shrug of the shoulders, which could provoke a continuation of this line of questioning. "Who had a right to be angry in your family?" In this way, the search for pertinent information becomes focussed.

If the therapist feels confident in the sense that something is ready to be revealed in the situation, even though nothing clear is coming directly from the client, it is possible to simply begin the constellation. There might be just two people at the beginning, a representative for the client and someone to represent the issue. The constellation then moves ahead on its own, and may reveal further information. Or, if the therapist feels concerned about unduly influencing the constellation, he or she may set aside any hunches or intuitions and continue the interview in hopes of discovering other pertinent information.

Any preconceptions on the part of the therapist about information provided by the client's system pose a risk. Does the therapist have a true sense of reality, or only associations? Associations from the therapist's personal reality may lead down the wrong path, or may provoke unfounded assertions, either of which undermines the client's trust. Such associative interpretations remain flat and lifeless and will quickly reveal themselves as unproductive when they are spoken, or by their effects on the group. If this happens, the therapist can later make appropriate corrections and try a different approach towards opening up a useful path. In my experience, clients won't follow a false lead in a constellation, and the representatives will also resist any such movement. If the path turns out to be fundamentally wrong, it may be necessary to break off the constellation and try again at some later time.

What is true for the client's presenting issue also holds true for all other information. Problems and events need not be described in great detail. Such descriptions are usually distracting and, in any case, somewhat biased. They detract from the effectiveness of a constellation. It is more effective for the client and the group when details of significant events arise surprisingly from the physical or verbal reactions of the representatives, instead of coming from the client to the group. Describing problems in excessive detail is one way of holding on to problems, and it deepens the reactivity. Detailed descriptions of events can have a hypnotic effect on both client and therapist. They reawaken old images and instead of relieving symptoms, they bring the terrible past to life again by renewing the same physical reactions. Sometimes they call up old defence mechanisms that have been used in the past to control the effects of these experiences.

The way in which a client shares information already tells the therapist something about the client's method of dealing with traumatic events. A client may weep openly while telling of tragic family events, but there may be a histrionic quality that makes an observer sceptical of this reaction. Some clients harden and others laugh when relating something horrible. Some reports tempt the listener into taking sides with one party, whereas others prompt only yawns. Therapists must remain aware of all these aspects and either share their impressions, or file them away at the back of their mind for future reference. The therapist cannot respond to any invitation to identify with the client's perspective, but must remain in a position of benevolent openness to aid the revealing and resolving movements in the family soul as a whole system.

Many clients I have already done one or more constellations, and this is also useful information for the therapist. It is useful to know the topics of previous constellations and perhaps what effects they had. The therapist is then better able to pay attention to new effects or new aspects of repeated dynamics, which might be resolved in the current constellation. It is not important to know anything about the process of a previous constellation or about the actions of any previous therapists. It is fruitless to enter into therapy processes that occurred in the past. It only leads towards feelings of superiority, or tempts one to try to do everything "better". Attention then shifts to the question of what should have been done, or to a competitive attitude, and away from the essentials of the moment. The therapist should focus as much as possible on what is needed for this client in this present situation, without judgemental evaluations of the past.

The immediacy of the process of gathering information is what helps to illuminate and clarify. In contrast to long-term therapies, in this approach, a therapist does not require detailed knowledge about events in the family, need not make extensive notes about such events, nor remember details beyond the information gathered during this first interview. If the therapist is thinking about what he or she knows about this client, it impairs the therapist's ability to observe and sense accurately, by distracting attention from what is needed at this moment to initiate a process of resolution. Sometimes, when a client has a question some time after a constellation, or is having difficulty coping with the experience of the constellation, I have a telephone session with the person. Often, very surprising new information comes up, precisely because I don't remember everything about the client, and I am free to react in a new and fresh way to the person and the issues.

The process of gathering information at the beginning and during a constellation is an integral part of the constellation process, not a preparation that has to be got out of the way. It serves the therapist's awareness, but also influences the path of action. It guides the client and connects the attention of the group with the dynamics of the "field at the soul level".

A constellation is a complete experience that begins the moment someone begins to contemplate doing a constellation and lasts until there are no further effects in the client's life.

Observers of family constellations will notice differences in therapists' timing for gathering information; depending on the situation, this may also vary for any one therapist. Generally, the basic question is whether new data will provide strength at a particular time, whether it fills a gap that needs bridging, whether it prompts a stagnant process to move on, whether it has some logic in terms of what is happening, and whether it has a direct and immediate effect when it is brought forth and understood. The initial interview is usually useful only up to the point when the therapist feels that a constellation is now possible.

Anything else can always be asked for later if necessary. In this way, information fits into the organic process of the constellation.

In some constellations, data from the client plays absolutely no role at all. In an advanced training group in Brazil, a woman who appeared to have African ancestry asked to do a constellation. When asked about her issue, she could only say that ever since she was able to remember, she had felt a deep pain in her chest. She said this in such a moving way, that a deep, empathetic feeling arose immediately in the entire group. The therapist was aware that if he asked for additional information at this point, the force of this single sentence would be dissipated. I will describe this moving constellation later, a constellation that developed solely through the reactions of the representatives and a few sparse interventions from the therapist, but no further information. The question of when or how much information is necessary is very open. There may be a complete interview at the beginning, a gradual process of information gathering during the constellation, or working with no actual information from the client.

The information needed emerges in a dialogic process between the client, the therapist, and the "field" forces of the constellation itself. This dialogue takes many diverse forms. Sometimes, it seems like tracking down information in the manner of a detective novel. Sometimes, it appears quietly through the images in the constellation. It develops continuously in new, unpredictable and unplanned ways, as do all movements of a constellation.

The Choice of Relationship System

The choice of which relationship system to set up is made by the therapist and is determined by the presenting issue and the more or less complete information from the interview. We live in various internal and external relationship systems simultaneously. The systems that exist in us and around us are not isolated from one another, but are interconnected in very complex ways. To result in clarifying and resolving effects, a constellation, just as any process in the soul, rests on limited, select segments of the entire relationship network.

One significant decision is whether to set up a constellation of the present family system, or that of the family of origin. The present family system is defined as the system in which a person is a husband, wife, father, or mother. The family of origin is the family system in which one is a son, daughter, grandson, granddaughter, nephew, or niece. If the client's issue has to do with a partner relationship or with the person's children, a constellation is set up of the present family. If the issue is related to the person's parents or to events that shaped the client's childhood, the family of origin is set up.

In a constellation of a present family system, if effects that originate with parents or grandparents become visible, part of the family of origin may be added to the constellation. Likewise, resolving dynamics in a constellation of the family of origin can be opened towards the future by including a current partner or child. Sometimes, parents and all their children are set up in the constellation, but sometimes, at least to start with, the constellation only includes the couple, or the client and one child, or the client with his or her parent or parents.

If, for example, the client's paternal grandfather committed suicide, the therapist might ask the client to set up only the father and the father's parents. If the client is suffering from a physical or behavioural condition, or from a constant or recurring emotional problem, the therapist may set up representatives for those symptoms in relation to the client. A constellation could begin with the position and movement of a single person – the client or someone else in the family. If a grandfather, for example, acted as a warden in a concentration camp during the war, his representatives might be placed facing representatives of prisoners, or murdered Jews.

The choice of relationship system and the extent of the representation is naturally a determining factor for the course of the constellation. The therapist has very few guidelines in this matter except that it is easier to begin with fewer people and expand when and where needed, rather than starting with a large system at the start. If representatives have been added and prove to be non-essential to the resolution, it is no problem to take them back out of the constellation again. The issue and facts will usually indicate a constellation of a particular relationship. Another general guideline is that when in doubt, whatever serves the future has priority over insight into the past.

The therapist need not think through a decision about which system or how many people will be included, but can trust the client's "family soul". It is difficult to describe and impossible to analyse how therapists feel the guidance of these greater forces of the soul, but it is one of the amazing, fundamental experiences of people who work with constellations. This "intuition" and a sense of being guided are processes we recognise from all aspects of our lives. In family constellations it contributes to the "method", but cannot substitute for technical skill and care. This intuition helps the therapist decide which system, which people, and/or which symptoms or qualities will be set up in a constellation.

Sometimes clients come into a group with a specific request, "I want to set up my family of origin, because..." This kind of set idea is usually problematic. If the client knew how to find the path to healing, he or she wouldn't be looking for help. Such prescriptions may also be an attempt to steer the constellation away from an issue that is "too hot". For example, people who are experiencing marital problems tend to look for causes in their family of origin because any resolution that appears in the couple's system is likely to bear consequences, perhaps a separation or maybe giving up an extra-marital relationship.

Sometimes, however, we are subjected to consequences in the present although the background of the difficulties lies buried in the family history of one partner or the other. It sometimes becomes clear why a relationship has failed only after a long period of time has passed, and after the consequences have already been suffered. Marriage counselling often takes a long time because by searching for background factors, we gain time and can perhaps postpone any need for action, or we can wait to feel certain about the right course of action. If a therapist has a sense that a client is scrutinising the past in order to avoid facing the present, it may be most helpful to avoid the distraction and lead the client towards a constellation of the system that will best serve appropriate action. However, insisting on a constellation of the present system is useless if it conflicts with the client's wishes. I have frequently had the experience of asking clients to set up their present family system, only to see them spontaneously choose representatives for their mother and father. It is clear in such cases that there was no inner readiness to look at the present family. When that happens, I have to interrupt the process and approach the issue in a different way at a later time. Regardless of which system the therapist chooses, it must be a decision the client can support if the constellation is to have any chance of success.

There was a young woman in a course who suffered from fears and anxiety. Her mother wanted her to do a constellation to find a resolution to these problems, and her mother had also come to stay at the hotel where the course was being held. When the woman asked to do this constellation, she also mentioned that her father had committed suicide when she was a young child. The therapist had her set up her family of origin, but the representatives were unable to feel their way into the system and the constellation had to be broken off. The woman was very disappointed and retorted angrily, "I told my mother I didn't want to do a constellation about my anxiety; I wanted to get clear about my relationship with my boyfriend!" At this point there was some real energy present that could carry a constellation. The following day, she did a very moving constellation of her relationship with her friend. The death of her father, her family history and her anxieties, all entered into the picture, but in this instance that was in the context of her love for her friend.

In this regard, I would like to comment again on the client's issue in relation to the choice of relationship system to work with. The formulation of the issue connects the client to the coming constellation experience and provides the desire for resolution that will carry the constellation process. The client's view of a problem, however, is limited. If a person were able to accurately describe what the problem was, the solution would be included in the description. Therefore, the therapist has to look beyond the client's formulation to what is needed for resolution. Clients seldom know what that might be, so it is the task of the therapist to identify this larger, usually unknown goal, and the client has to remain open to this process. This is one way the therapist serves the client. The depth and extent of the effects of a constellation are often determined by our ability to overcome the limitations of our preconceptions and beliefs. At the end of a recent group, a woman said, "You had me set up something completely different from what I originally wanted. I am not yet clear about my constellation, but I feel great. It has been a long time since I have felt so much confidence in my life."

The Choice of Representatives

The normal practice is for clients to choose their own representatives for the constellation. This supports the feeling that the constellation is truly the client's own. Choosing representatives and placing them in spatial relationship to one another allows someone to express a very personal, inner picture.

The constellation process begins when the client is asked to choose representatives. This selection should be done briskly, without set ideas about particular people or any special criteria. The client, the therapist, and the group must remain quiet, attentive, and centred during the process. The "field" for the coming event is created during the selection of representatives and their entry into the working space. (There are "invisible" constellations, which I will not describe in detail here, in which the therapist and the client remain sitting next to each other, without representatives being brought in. The therapist becomes aware of some aspect of a relationship – for example a mother's relationship to her aborted baby – and initiates a restorative influence on the relationship simply with quiet comments or healing inner images.)

Representatives have to be willing to give themselves over to a role, and it should be made clear that they are free to refuse if they don't feel able to participate in someone else's system at that particular moment, or if they feel a sense of anxiety about the role they are being asked to take over. Sometimes, a representative may not have completely finished with a previous role or experience and is not yet ready to move into another. When people agree to be representatives, they should leave any and all distractions outside the constellation, even including extraneous clothing, such as a conspicuous head covering. Energy must be free to flow and not be interrupted by something like gum chewing. The representatives' task is to make themselves available physically and mentally for the role and for influences from the relationship system.

It is not absolutely necessary for a client to personally choose the representatives. The process of a constellation will flow regardless of the individual characteristics of representatives – at least that is a basic assumption of family constellation work, which has been borne out by experience (Schlöter, 2005). The physical appearance of a representative plays no role in regards to a particular place in the system or the ability to feel into a role. To take over the role of "mother" one need not be a particular size, age, or appearance. The advantage of working with representatives is precisely that they are *not* like the family members, and their feelings will reflect more essential movements, free of characterisation and encumbrance. They are able to discern essentials of the situation that would be difficult for the actual family members to attend to because of the excess of information and interaction, and their personal closeness to each other. The more random the choice of representatives, the freer they are to reveal what is essential, because they are not subject to the conscious connections.

Someone who has served as a representative in a number of constellations will notice great differences in feelings in various roles and will be familiar with the experience of being flooded by feelings and sensations that are totally unknown from his or her personal life. The systemic forces and the "field" of the constellation have more powerful effects than the personal nature of the representatives. Choosing representatives without intention and without comment, but simply according to the feeling of the moment, frees the representatives to react exclusively to the systemic forces, and also leaves the client open to what is new and unexpected, rather than a repertoire limited by intention and expectation.

When I say that a client should rely on feelings to select representatives, it is implicitly understood that many subliminal cues will guide the choice, and it is only superficially "random". Representatives often find that they are repeatedly chosen for similar roles, for example, always as a father or a deserted lover, or a child who died prematurely. Unconscious motivations in the choice of appropriate representatives do not falsify a constellation, but rather, quite the opposite, they deepen it. The only thing that is really necessary is for the client's selection and the representatives' acceptance to be free from conscious intention, considerations, and associations. If the therapist sees that a representative is caught up in a personal process, either in entering into the role or during the constellation, the client or the therapist can choose a different representative for this role. Normally, however, the systemic forces are so powerful that representatives are able to set aside their own personal input for the duration of the constellation.

Therapists often choose the representatives, perhaps to spare the client interruptions or distractions during the constellation. This can relieve the client of the weight of choice, or make clear the random aspect of the process, or it may be that the therapist senses some uncertainty in the client. The therapist may prefer to have an experienced, reliable representative take on a particularly difficult role, someone whose capacity to feel their way into a role and express feelings is already known. Sometimes, the therapist might simply ask who in the group would like to be a representative. This offers people who have not been chosen the chance to have an experience of being a representative.

It is always possible to find reasons why a particular representive is chosen. Those reasons, however, are not as important as feelings, intuition, and a sense of being guided. What is most important is for the client to have the feeling that family members, symptoms, and a relationship system are available through the representatives in a congruent way, even if that way is sometimes surprising and unexpected. Of course, it is very important for the selection process and the placement of the representatives to take place in an atmosphere of peace and harmony between the therapist, client, and representatives. There should be no sense of resistance, but a deep trust in the guiding force of the soul of the client and the family.

The Constellation

When the representatives have been chosen, the therapist asks the client to place them in a spatial relationship to one another, based on a feeling of where the "right" place is. The client must be centred, and the placement done with utmost respect for the family members who are being represented, as well as for the representatives. The positioning is not dependent upon a particular time frame, and is not a result of logical thinking or a preconceived image. It is done without comment and with no instructions as to gestures or posture.

If the therapist notices that the client seems to be setting up a constellation in accordance with some previous picture, as if it had been thought out in advance, the therapist draws attention to this process and may ask the client to start over again. When people are very quick to set up the representatives and seem rather superficial, they can be asked to collect themselves, get grounded and to proceed with care and attention. If the client seems disconnected and uninvolved with the placement process, the therapist breaks off the constellation, because there is something preventing this client from entering into the constellation, or the family.

> A single woman of about thirty seemed to have a very aggressive attitude in the group. When she set up a constellation of her family of origin, she hustled the representatives into their places with such a lack of care that the therapist broke off the constellation and told the woman he could not work with her in this manner. The woman became very angry, but stayed on to the end of the seminar. About a year later, she came to

another group wanting to do a constellation of her family of origin, but again was very aggressive in her manner. This time she was a bit more careful and respectful with the representatives, but the representatives just shrugged because they could not feel their way into their roles. The therapist broke off this constellation as well, and the woman was again very angry. As before, however, she remained till the end of the group. A few weeks later, she phoned the therapist asking for a short private session. When she arrived, she seemed quite different from the previous encounters. She said that her mother had died and she had inherited her mother's house. In cleaning out the attic she had found some old papers that indicated that her grandfather had had an extra-marital affair and his lover got pregnant. The client's grandmother had paid off the mother of the child with the stipulation that the child could never have any contact with their family. The therapist indicated the significance of such an event and suggested that the woman get in contact with her newly discovered aunt. Two weeks later, the woman came for another session. This time, she seemed light-hearted. She said that she had located her aunt very easily and had called her. The aunt was apparently extremely hostile. The young woman, however, looked radiant and her earlier aggressive attitude had evaporated. The therapist commented that it was no wonder the aunt was angry, since she had been sold out of her family. The therapist recommended that the woman stay in touch with her aunt. "I planned to do that in any case," replied the woman, and left happily.

When a client asks whether the family should be set up as they are now or as they used to be, what needs to be emphasised is the "time-lessness" of a constellation. The nature of the soul, and therefore a constellation, has effects that are not related to time. The living and the dead are all equally present, and we cannot tell in advance which events and fates are still alive and active in a family. Pictures, by their very nature, capture an entire story in a single moment, compressing time and removing events from the reciprocal complexities of cause and effect. Constellations present pictures and images in the same way. Because they portray processes, time plays a role as well, but in a very compressed form, so we can move easily between past, present, and future moments.

Occasionally, a time orientation may be deliberately introduced in order to look at connections between sequential relationship systems. For example, a therapist might ask a woman to begin with a constellation of her first husband, herself, and their child. When the significant dynamics in that first marriage have become clear, the client adds her present husband and her children from the second marriage. Here too, we benefit from one of the advantages of constellations, in that complex relationship connections that extend over time and space can be portrayed in a compressed picture in a way that would be impossible to express with words.

Most of the time, people set up constellations in an appropriate manner without much instruction or explanation from the therapist. Sometimes a few guidelines are needed, such as: "Set it up without any specific time in mind. Set it up without any preconceived image in mind. Place the representatives in relationship to one another in a way that reflects the reality of your inner image. Follow your feelings. Trust your heart and your soul."

It may be useful to provide a bit of instruction about how to move representatives. "It works best if you hold representatives by their upper arms or shoulders, either from the front or from the back. Move them to their places without saying anything and without giving them any instructions. Move them in a way that allows them to feel secure." The therapist watches to see that the client places each and every representative. Sometimes a representative is simply left standing where they happened to end up during the selection process. When the therapist draws attention to this fact, the client might say something like, "Oh he's already in the right place." The client is asked to also place this representative, exactly in the same manner as the others. Usually this results in only a minor movement, such as a change of direction, but that can be crucial for the representative's ability to get a sense of the role.

In the main, the therapist leaves the placement process up to the client, and uses this time to pull back and concentrate on his or her own awareness and impressions of the process. An attentive focus from the group supports the placement process. If the group begins to be restless it is usually a sign that the client is not completely centred in the process, that the roles are not clear, or that the "field" is not developing for some reason. The therapist can draw attention to this phenomenon and perhaps comment that something seems to be amiss. The client might suddenly remember an important person that has been left out, or some pertinent information. When these are taken into consideration, they may give the constellation the necessary strength and focus. It may be, that the constellation has to be broken off, but new starting point might be found at a later time, after the needed strength has had time to develop.

The group's reactions sometimes belong to the constellation. I have had many experiences where people in a group all began whispering, often about who is representing whom in the constellation. Something of importance then often emerges – for example, perhaps that one child in the family has a different father and the fact has been concealed. Confusion in the group, among the representatives, or in the therapist may reflect some confusion in the system. The group sometimes react to hidden truths or inconsistencies as if they were the real environment of the family. When a client gets confused in choosing a representative, perhaps placing his mother's representative as his sister without noticing the shift, the therapist usually has to break off the constellation. If it were to continue, the client's confusion would be a burden to the representatives and impinge upon their awareness.

During the process of setting up the constellation, the therapist attempts to take in even the tiniest reactions and movements from the first moment on. He or she retains these impressions as possible indications of what to look at in this relationship system.

Occasionally, the client may not feel capable of setting up the representatives. If there is a clear picture of the client's system, based on data and impressions, the therapist can set up the constellation according to this image. Of course this carries a risk, and it only works if the client's spontaneous reaction is, "Yes. That's exactly right!" Most of the time, it is only possible for the therapist to set up the constellation if it involves a relationship system in which the inner image from the client is not of primary importance. For example, it might be a constellation of a representative for the client and a representative for the client's mother, facing each other; or representatives for the client and death; or a grandmother and the man who raped her. It would be possible for a therapist to set up a constellation with representatives of countries – for example, the client's mother's homeland, the father's homeland at some distance, and the client, or a representative for the client, standing in the middle or in front of them.

I mentioned a woman earlier who was experiencing a sense of panic because she believed that her father might be a murderer because he was ostensibly an engineer involved in the construction of the V2 missiles. The therapist asked the client to choose a representative for her father and the therapist chose 10 representatives for the English victims of the V2 bombings. He had them lie on the floor next to each other and placed the father in front of them. In a case like this, the soul dynamics cannot be illustrated in a constellation of relationships that visually represents the person's family.

In many "big" constellations that have to do with war or with victim-perpetrator relationships, constellations that extend beyond family connections, the therapist uses simple spatial relationships to reveal the forces of the soul. This is also an option when dealing with ancestors over many generations, or with the soul's relationship to an illness or symptomatic behaviour, or when working with large concepts such as life and death. Often, in these constellations there is little or no information about actual persons or their relationship to each other, so there are no "realistic" pictures of the relationships. In classical family constellations it is usually important for the client to provide the image for the constellation and the subliminal information needed to move the constellation forward.

I often use the following metaphor to illustrate the constellation process to groups. It is as though the attention that is focussed on the client allows the group soul to collect, like a magnetic force field. We can make a magnetic force field visible within certain spatial limitations, by strewing metal filings, which will arrange themselves along the lines of magnetic forces. Likewise, the representatives in a "soul field" respond to the forces present with their gestures, movements and words. In this way, the dynamics of the soul are visible even in one person alone, without a constellation of a relationship system. In that sense, it is not of great importance whether the therapist or the client is the one who sets up the constellation. It is clear that this is a metaphorical explanation, and does not presume to be a physical explanation.

The Constellation Image

As each person is placed in the constellation, an image and a force field are created. Perhaps the most important moment of constellation work occurs when the client, the therapist, the representatives, and the group observer-participants surrender to the effects of this image and the associated force field. The client, the therapist and the group remain outside the constellation field, while the representatives are inside it.

After the representatives have been placed in a constellation, there follows a phase of collected quiet as the representatives feel their way into their roles and notice any physical sensations and feelings, or an urge to move in some particular way or say something. The therapist uses this time to take in the image that has been set up and feel its impact. More precisely, the therapist lets the field of the relationship system work. Without getting caught up in any details, the therapist notices the first, often minimal physical reactions of the representatives including impulses towards movement, restlessness, changes in posture, or a particular visual orientation (such as looking down at the floor, up at the ceiling or off into the distance).

At the same time, the therapist pays attention to any inner reactions, feelings, or sensitivities that arise in response to these images. We might call these reactions the therapist's hypothesis about the reality of the relationship. In fact, however, these first hypotheses often take shape in pictures and sensory awareness. There may be the first inkling of a "truth" (in the sense of the old Greek work "aletheia", a state of not being concealed). Therapists allow themselves to be moved by the family soul or the "greater" soul, the system in the constellation. As far as possible, the therapist remains in a state of "emptiness" (which is, of course, only relative), and is moved by whatever is revealed and whatever has an impact. At the same time, the connection to the client and his or her experience must remain as open as possible.

This is often the most difficult moment for the therapist because there is not yet anything to be done and the direction of the constellation is not yet clear. This is when a therapist may be tempted to think about the constellation and the available data, and look for meaningful connections, or to contemplate what might come next. There may be a pressing feeling of responsibility, as if the success or failure of the constellation depended upon the therapist's actions alone. There might be some anxiety about the representatives' first reactions. Sometimes, a therapist might even feel tempted to start looking immediately for the safe territory of a resolution.

This moment, more than any other, calls for what Bert Hellinger called "phenomenological observing", observing without prior assumptions, without intention, without fear, and without love (in the sense of lovingly wanting to help). This first phase of the constellation also marks the initial participation in the core dynamics moving this family. As the therapist and representatives allow themselves to be more and more deeply affected by the constellation, gradually becoming aware of the hidden dynamics of the family, a profound feeling of awe and gratitude arises that one has been allowed to participate in this process. This first, brief, quiet moment has great significance for the on-going process of the constellation. It is like a seed that carries hints of what it will become, but does not yet reveal itself in a recognisable form. It creates a fertile space in which the soul of the client and of the family can reveal itself.

This all may sound a bit mystical to some readers, and you can be assured that this first experience of the effects of a constellation is not always marked by deep, powerful or moving dynamics. Sometimes one has the feeling that absolutely nothing is happening, and the strength and dynamics of a constellation often develop later, in the following steps. This is a common occurrence when some pivotal person has not yet been put into the constellation, or when critical information is still missing. Also, constellation images do not always touch deep places immediately and sometimes, everyone's reactions remain empty. It sometimes seems like the sensible action would be to break off the constellation when the images are weak and inert, but it is worth the effort to stay with the process and trust that something will emerge.

Occasionally, representatives exhibit bizarre reactions right from the start of a constellation.

> A Dutch man set up a constellation of his family of origin, but before he could even move the representatives into position, they began to giggle and then broke out into loud laughter and could not calm down. This had a powerful impact on the client and he felt completely bewildered. The therapist considered breaking off the constellation, but followed his inner inclination to observe the phenomenon a bit further. Suddenly, he was struck by an image of a wedding party, so he asked the man what had happened at his parents' wedding. The man reported that his aunt had once told him about his parents' wedding reception, where a woman showed up with her 20-year-old daughter. She marched up to the new bride, in front of all the guests, and showed her a ring on her daughter's finger. She told the woman that the groom had given her daughter that ring with a promise to marry her. Upon hearing this, all the representatives were suddenly very still. The therapist chose representatives for the woman and her daughter and led them before the representatives of the family. The two women, who were probably ridiculed in the actual situation, could now be met with respect and empathy. Their anger, pain, and shame could be treated with compassion and they could be acknowledged as belonging to the system.
>
> Another man, a rather light-hearted, scattered sort of a fellow, set up a constellation of his parents and all five children in the family. Based on

information from the initial interview, the therapist had asked about the father's previous relationships. As a result, the father's previous fiancée was also included in the constellation from the start. As a young, would-be baker with no capital, the father had roamed around looking for a suitable wife. He found a woman who had a bakery but after they got engaged, the man wandered off again. The client knew nothing more than that.

The man set up his family in a row with this fiancée facing them. They were barely in place before they were all bent double with laughter. The representative for the fiancée was laughing so uncontrollably that she had to leave the room to go to the toilet. The therapist felt obliged to break off the constellation. The client phoned his father, who then told him that the young woman with the bakery had turned out to be insane, which is why the he had taken to his heels as fast as possible.

It is rare that representatives have such extreme reactions, but there are some reactions that commonly appear when the representatives are in position. These include: falling to the floor, turning away, taking a few steps away, making a fist, looking upwards or covering their face with their hands. These kinds of initial reactions usually bear some significance. As a rule, however, the therapist will guide representatives to exercise restraint with large movements so that there is ample time to observe the constellation picture and allow the movements to unfold solely from the strength of the constellation.

Dynamics of the Soul

The impact of this constellation image on the representatives initiates a process that lies at the heart of constellation work. It reveals the soul dynamics of this relationship field, allowing significant events and connections, both internal and external, to come to light. This process lasts between five minutes and an hour, but usually takes about twenty to forty minutes. It embodies the essentials of content, method, and fundamental principles that inform all constellation work. A more comprehensive discussion of the dynamics of the soul can be found in the chapter "*Bonds and Resolution*".

The therapist's interventions combine with the dynamics of the constellation itself to lend constellations their individual, unique colour and produce complexities that continue to surprise even experienced therapists. For clients, the only thing of any significance is what touches them and provides insight into essential, systemic realities, and what reveals previously hidden aspects and potential resolution and healing. The client is free to simply observe what is there, with no demands to do anything, to understand or believe anything, or to make any decisions about a future course of action.

Clients may participate directly at some point in the course of a constellation, in order to have the physical experience of their own place. This could be a brief dialogue with parents, or experiencing the effects of a ritual such as standing in front of a line of ancestors, or bowing down to parents. Sometimes, the therapist may feel that a client needs to look at the way things actually are, or that the person needs to personally speak a sentence of resolution ("I will always love you as my father") or to physically express a symbolic gesture (bowing down).

In making such a decision, the therapist is assuming a heavy responsibility, and such directive action has often been criticised in the public forum. If it is not absolutely right on the mark and, does not bring about the hoped-for resolution, it makes the group uneasy. In the end, however, the observer/participants and the representatives will align themselves on the side of the client if there is any impropriety. Direction from a therapist elicits supporting energy only when the actions are in complete harmony with the client and the client's family. Normally, a client is free to take in whatever happens in his or her own way, which supports the individuality of that person's response.

The therapist can choose from two basic approaches. The representatives can be left free to follow whatever impulses they experience within the developing "field", or the therapist can make interventions by re-positioning representatives, asking them to move in some particular way, or by adding additional representatives. The client may be asked to give feedback, the therapist may make comments about what he or she sees, or may ask some or all of the representatives to report their experience.

In reality, what usually happens is the result of a mixture of all of these. No constellation proceeds completely free of all influence from a therapist, even if it is only a decision about who will be included at the start, and when the constellation begins and ends. The therapist participates in the shaping of whatever appears in the constellation process in concert with the client's soul and the realities of the relationship system. He or she may take a role similar to that of an orchestra conductor, shaping music that has already been written, or like that of a director helping actors to perform a play that has been written by someone else.

Given the complexity of the constellation process, it is useful to differentiate between two fundamental approaches to setting up a constellation: "movements of the soul" and "orders of love", two terms that have become part of the vocabulary of constellation work, and also the two concepts of "image" and "language".

Constellations Using Movements of the Soul

"Movements of the soul" as a method refers to the freedom for representatives to follow their own impulses within the constellation field. Classic constellation methods emphasise the role of the therapist in shaping and ordering the impulses that arise, and in naming dynamics that appear. The more recent development of this other, largely silent, procedure, in which the therapist does not guide towards resolution, has added an impressive depth to many constellations. However, verbalisation and re-positioning representatives are also expressions of movements of the soul, and free movement and frugal use of verbal communication have always been important elements of constellation work.

What has sometimes been seen as a radical departure on the part of Bert Hellinger into these "movements of the soul" has stirred up many questions and considerable unrest amongst constellation leaders. "Does permitting representatives to move freely lead to an overly dramatic result that is more of a burden to the client than a release?" "Without the neutral overview of a therapist, don't the personal issues of representatives slip into the constellations?" "Is there not a danger that a constellation will develop its own dynamics that are not visibly or reliably connected to the client's relationship system?" "Doesn't this open the flood gates for any and every interpretation and to a lack of clarity?" "How is one to understand the movements of the representatives without any verbalised commentary?"

On the other hand, we have experienced constellations that, through these "movements of the soul", have such power and such powerful effects that almost no one can avoid being touched. I would like to include the example of Fatima, the Brazilian woman I mentioned earlier, who reported "a deep pain in my chest" as her issue.

The powerful effect of this single sentence, the deep pain reflected in the client's eyes, and a feeling as though the roots of this woman sitting next to me reached down into the earth, prompted me to choose two representatives for her constellation: a representative for her, and one for her pain. I placed them in the centre of the working space with the observing group in a semi-circle around them. They were facing each other at a distance of about one metre. I left the next movements up to them. After a few moments "Pain" opened her arms as if she were inviting Fatima to come to her. Fatima's representative, however, slowly shrank back in horror, her eyes opened wide and her arms stretched out defensively. She crept back step-by-step until she was at the very edge of the group. There, she stood motionless as "Pain" let her arms fall to her sides.

For a while, nothing happened. Then, "Fatima" became restless and began to breathe in deep, irregular breaths. She clutched her breast, turning her head from side to side as if she were seeking something, and cried, "I can't stand any more!" There was no response to this sentence. She sat down on the floor, then stood up again but dropped again to the floor. She began to weep and called out, "Won't anyone help me?" There was no response. She wept silently for a long time until, suddenly, she froze and, covering her face with her hands, she called out in a tone of deep resignation, "So many dead!"

The client sat quietly weeping as she watched from her place next to me. When she heard this sentence, however, she seemed to shiver. I felt a ripple up my own spine and there was a feeling of breathless tension in the group. In response to this, I randomly chose ten representatives from the group to represent the dead. They were asked to lie on the floor within the working space in any way that felt right to them. The men and women placed themselves so that "Pain" was encircled by them, and "Fatima" sat on the outside. "Pain" looked peacefully around at them in a friendly and attentive manner, but did nothing. "Fatima" initially shrugged her shoulders indifferently, but then reared up, clutching her breast again screaming, "It hurts so much!" After a while she looked around and again asked, very quietly, "Won't anyone help me?"

Without speaking, I chose a representative for Fatima's mother and placed her on the edge of this field of death facing "Fatima". No one but myself knew who this person was meant to be, not even the representative herself. "Fatima" looked longingly at this woman, but the woman did not react. She remained motionless and expressionless exactly where I had placed her. I again intervened and asked "Pain" to leave the circle of the dead and lead "Fatima" to each of the dead representatives. She did this and "Fatima" willingly allowed herself to be led and supported by "Pain". In a long, touching process she bid each of the dead goodbye. Sometimes she moaned, sometimes she wept, and sometimes she embraced them warmly. The dead also reacted in various ways; some smiled in a friendly manner, others wept, and some clung to her for a while until they became peaceful.

In the group, too, many people sat with tears in their eyes. It was as if they were all experiencing something that bound them together in their individual inner images in an empathetic solidarity with Fatima and her unknown fate, perhaps images stemming from their own personal memories. They were participating in an experience that may have been Brazilian, but was perhaps wholly human, that seemed to extend far beyond direct personal experience.

As "Pain" and "Fatima" came to the last dead person, something unexpected happened. This woman looked angrily at "Fatima", who refused to approach her. She shook her head and said, "No!" The woman jumped up and moved aggressively towards the screaming "Fatima" as if she wanted to strangle her. With a gentle touch, I asked the dead woman to lie down again, which she reluctantly did. "Pain" bent down to this dead woman and took her gently, lovingly in her arms. It felt almost as if an evil spirit was being released from this woman. She wept heartbreakingly until she finally became calm and closed her eyes. "Pain" reached out her hand in invitation to the dumbfounded "Fatima", who went to sit on the floor with "Pain", gently touched the dead woman, and let out a deep breath. "Pain" stood up and nodded encouragingly for "Fatima" to follow her. "Fatima", however, remained seated, saying, "I am dead tired."

The angry outburst of the last dead woman had occurred right in front of where the client was sitting, and she, too, had reacted with shock. Now she looked over at her representative and nodded. She could well feel this seemingly never-ending exhaustion. I felt as if there was something still missing that might help Fatima to take a step towards resolution, so I added two more representatives. I put "Death" near the dead, and "Life" facing her, but on the outside of the field of the dead. "Fatima" understood the implicit invitation to make her decision and she again shook her head and said, "I cannot." Then, she gathered her strength and with the help of "Pain", she stood up with great effort and looked around. She looked uncertainly at "Life", and took a few steps in that direction, holding "Pain's" hand. There, she stopped and said, "I can't make it."

At this point, the representative for her mother moved for the first time. She came up gently behind "Fatima" and put her arm around her daughter. "Fatima" leaned against her, closed her eyes and sighed deeply. After a short while, I ended the constellation with this picture and asked the representatives to return to their seats. Slowly, the trance state dissolved in the group. The client appeared completely calm and she turned to me with tears in her eyes, took my hand, and said with her whole heart, "Thank you!"

We have no way of knowing what happened here, but scarcely a person among those present felt untouched by the power of this constellation. We could see the "movement of a soul" and somehow comprehend it without understanding exactly what the constellation was showing us about this client and her systemic reality. The interpreter told me during the break that some people in the group shared a suspicion that this had to do with a "slave" history. Except for the client and her mother, who was never explicitly identified, no family members were set up in this constellation. There was only a physical symptom, unknown dead people, and life and death. Whether or not the dead woman who reacted so violently or the other dead people actually represented concrete individuals from this family is completely unknown. The client was never asked about it and the constellation did not develop from any concrete information about the client or her family history. The only information we had was what could be experienced in the course of the constellation, and the meaning of the experience remains with the client. We do not know what connections the client made to her own family history or her personal situation. There is a very moving anonymity.

How do forces with such an impact develop in a constellation? What do we think about the therapist's interventions? Who or what is in charge here? Would the client have been as involved and touched if there were no connection between the constellation and her personal life? Could representatives invent reactions like that, and if so, would it prompt such a resonance in the other representatives, the client, the therapist and the group? These questions arise in the immediate impressions during such a constellation, but they have to be carefully considered in later reflection. As yet, we have few answers that are sufficient to still our desire for explanations.

When we have experienced many constellations, with their wide variety of beginnings and progression, we can scarcely escape the feeling that we can see "soul" in operation, within a wider or narrower range, and with varying degrees of comprehensibility. It feels as if we are being allowed to participate in the compressed essence of human experience, something we rarely experience in our everyday lives. This is precisely what makes it so important that constellations not be used for self-interests, for cultural or religious constructs, and certainly not for entertainment (even though they sometimes turn out to have these effects). The concern must remain with the fate of a client, and a potentially resolving, healing, and satisfying process that will continue to work in that person's life.

Perhaps Fatima's constellation can help to clarify how and when it is appropriate to do a constellation of the "movements of the soul"; that is, namely, when we are looking less at the relationship system of a family and more at symptoms, feelings, illness, or life and death, which reach beyond an immediate family process into the arena of societal events, such as war, injustice, or "good and evil". Of course, even in a "purely" family constellation, it makes sense to incorporate free movements of the representatives and the soul, particularly when there is missing information or when the therapist has the feeling that the physical expressions of the representatives are offering more depth and are more informative than their verbal comments. Words may be more exact, but they are narrower in scope than pictures.

Generally, one can say that we more often turn to "movements of the soul" when there is less information available. When the therapist's experience and understanding of basic relationship structures leads towards a more direct path to resolution in order, then this is the more usual route. For example, if there is conflict in a man-woman relationship revolving around a child from a previous marriage who has been adopted by the current husband, a therapist with an understanding of the orders of relationships will be able to contribute to a resolution. In such a case, the therapist is at the same human level as the client and family members. When death, war, illness, or such issues are involved, the therapist is not on the same plane and human choice cannot solve the problem. These are forces that are larger than any person and beyond the scope of resolution suggested by a therapist. They are certainly beyond the sphere where an individual could control the movements. Here, the therapist has to trust in the field of the soul that supports the client and trust that the forces revealed through the representatives will show what is bound, and also what might bring resolution. A therapist's experience and intuition are, of course, still valuable and certain images and an overview might give indications of what would help, but this is always tempered by caution and guided solely by this greater perspective (whatever name you might give to that).

Representatives can only express what they, as individuals, are able to draw from the field of the soul, and what they can "weigh", or "measure". This "scientific" process of subjecting experience to objective checks and balances protects representatives of "supra-human forces" from being tempted to go beyond what is humanly comprehensible. The whole constellation process, regardless of what forces are represented, remains a perfectly normal dialogue between ordinary people. This common-sense orientation gives the therapist the right and obligation, to intervene in service of what is useful and tolerable for the client, even though "movements of the soul" are carrying the constellation. As said, this demands care and caution, and a keen sensitivity to what is seen, heard, and sensed, with openness to the unexpected. It requires a humble respect for what is "greater".

Constellations Using Orders of Love

In Chapter 2, I included details of a constellation that followed the structures of the "orders of love". In this kind of a constellation, the therapist intervenes much more directly to guide the representatives (and sometimes the client as well), in keeping with the facts provided by the client and the therapist's understanding of the processes of resolution. These constellations rely to a greater degree on verbal communication.

The representatives are asked to feel their way into their roles and their positions, at first without any movements. If the representatives are really into their roles, as is usually the case, the therapist begins by asking them about their experience. If people are not familiar with constellation work, particularly at the beginning of a seminar, they may need reassurance and encouragement to fully trust their feelings and perceptions and to express them openly, without worrying about protecting someone's feelings. Most people are able to do this quite easily.

Once in a while, a representative will respond, not from the role, but with general thoughts and ideas, for example, an opinion about a father in such a situation, or something that he or she feels might be helpful for the client. Sometimes a representative may simply describe the physical situation, "I am standing behind my wife and everyone is in front of me" and remain focussed on the most superficial level. Usually, the only correction needed is a bit of encouragement from the therapist.

If the client's parents and siblings have been set up in a constellation but there are no clear dynamics visible, the therapist begins the questioning with the parents and continues with the eldest child first and then other children according to age. If, however, there is a representative who exhibits a conspicuous reaction, the therapist begins with that impulse. It is not necessary, and may even be unhelpful, to question each and every representative, particularly in a large system.

As soon as there is any feedback that indicates an important movement, the therapist follows the flow of that energy and begins changing the positioning of the representatives. If this is not done, the energy may dissipate, or the constellation may become overwhelmed by too much information and can become confusing. In any case, it is easier to use questions to keep a large amount of data organised and moving along a constructive path, than to allow a large number of representatives, for instance, a family with six children, to move in an unrestricted way. Constellations of any kind generally suffer if too much information is presented all at the same time.

When representatives are asked for feedback and reactions, the client will probably be able to recognise his or her family in the wealth of information. The feedback process should not be too tightly restricted, but rather permitted to develop freely, because the experience of seeing strangers develop familiar symptoms and reactions can be of great help to the client.

A therapist cannot possibly work with all relevant relationships and all the currents of fate in a system and still keep focussed on a resolution for the client. It is generally easier to follow the first dynamics that appear and to question additional representatives later if the first movements prove to be unfruitful or confusing, rather than attempting to filter a vast a flood of information to find what is essential for the client and for resolution.

It sometimes happens that a representative cannot feel anything very strongly, which is information that has to be taken seriously, and not interpreted as a lack of sensitivity on the part of that representative. We are frequently confronted with examples of this kind of response in our everyday communication. Consider the woman who comes to a counselling session complaining that her husband has no emotions; further investigation may reveal that the husband is not lacking in feelings and sensitivities, but is reluctant to let them show.

Some overly verbal representatives need to be encouraged to restrict their responses to what is truly of essence, in a brief and simple way. When a representative exhibits strong feelings or a spontaneous physical reaction, the therapist follows these non-verbal cues. They often have depth and impact and could lose some of their power in a verbalised form.

On the other hand, words help to elucidate the meaning of non-verbal reactions, when there is something that is unclear. Every time a representative looks at the floor, it does not necessarily mean there is a dead person there. Sometimes, the representative is feeling a sense of shame or melancholy, or perhaps simply does not want to look at anyone. A brief description of the feeling or body reaction helps to clarify the situation.

If a representative says something that seems to contradict the therapist's impressions of the visible dynamics, the therapist has to trust his or her own neutral observations and feelings. The reactions can be filed away until a more appropriate time later, or the conflicting impressions can be brought up at once to observe the reactions of the client and the representatives. The burden of responsibility is lightened for the representatives by the awareness and observations of the therapist. Obviously, it would be very non-productive for the therapist to get into a dispute with a representative about the "right" reaction. In any case, the movements of the constellation usually eventually correct and clarify any interpretations.

There are constellations in which the representatives, just as the actual family members, get into arguments with one another. That can be very informative initially, but as in reality, it can also distract attention from what is really essential. The constellation then threatens to become a role-play and pulls the representatives away from their connection to the client's soul and the client's family. This generally leads to reactions that make a connection to the family system increasingly difficult.

Some representatives seem to feel left out if they are not asked to share their reactions, and they may insist on being heard. This, too, may stem from a typical reaction in the system. Nonetheless, the therapist will normally ask them to hold back for a bit, reassuring them that everyone will get a chance to share what is important for the client at an appropriate time.

No matter how meaningfully individual representatives express their feelings and reactions, they are still standing inside the system and cannot possibly have an overview and orientation to the entire system. The therapist is in a better position to do this because he or she is looking at the relationship structures of the family as a whole in the context of the facts that are known. Maintaining an overview of the system as a whole is the fundamental task of the therapist.

As the representatives are giving their feedback, the therapist also observes the client's reactions. The client may be asked to comment on the representatives' feedback, or asked if there seems to be any personal significance in their comments. Sometimes, the therapist feels uncertain about the representatives' reports, or perhaps notices some discrepancy between their feedback and the client's reactions. Generally, however, the client will probably confirm the representatives' feedback.

Occasionally, there are reactions or comments that appear foreign to the client. If the work were to continue at this point, the constellation would bypass the client completely. The client might say something like, "That's not my family at all," or "That is completely foreign to me." Even if the reactions of the representatives are right on target, and the client's view distorted, there is no value in continuing on if the client has no connection to the constellation. How useful is a truth that cannot be taken in?

The therapist goes with the verbal and non-verbal reactions of the representatives, information provided about this family, and personal reactions, to guide the constellation. This guidance includes changing the positions of representatives, adding representatives for any people who have not been previously included, and repeatedly asking for feedback from the representatives, until the constellation reaches the point where the critical relationships are clear in relation to the client's initial problem. Step by step, the burdens that are weighing upon the group soul are revealed and it becomes clear which dynamics are firmly bound to a movement of fate, and what movements are pressing for conclusions or healing.

When the orders of love are supporting the movements of the constellation, the challenge for the therapist is to trust what actually appears in terms of the love, strength, and truth of the system, and not to fall into the trap of following a rigid set of rules. It does not present a major obstacle if an erroneous movement should break the flow of the constellation or interrupt the process of revealing entanglements and resolution. The therapist can make corrections and return to the path of the constellation. False turns are quickly detectable if the therapist is paying close attention to the reactions of the representatives, the client, the group, and his or her own personal resonance. When a constellation gets stuck, it is most often due to insufficient information that would support a forward movement, and only rarely a result of the therapist's lack of awareness.

A woman in a group was complaining of a feeling of being cut off from her love for her husband, and a similar feeling in her relationship with her mother. When questioned, she reported that her grandmother had died of tuberculosis when her mother, the youngest in the family, was three years old. The woman's mother was added to the constellation of the present family with the client's husband and children, and the grandmother (the mother's mother) placed on the floor in front of her. All the representatives became rigid and stiff. It was immediately clear that this event in the family had weighed on the following two generations. The therapist had the client's mother say a few sentences to the grandmother, in hopes that it would thaw her frozen grief over this early loss, but her rigidity remained firmly in place. The client then also mentioned that her grandmother had spent the two years before her death quarantined in a sanatorium. With this revelation, both the mother and grandmother simultaneously broke into tears, and embraced, sobbing. This additional information, that finally broke the ice, made it clear that it was not only the grandmother's death, but also the preceding separation between the child and her mother that had caused an interruption in the reaching-out movement.

When the therapist is working with the orders of love in a constellation, the processes of uncovering and resolving go hand in hand. These steps include verbal and non-verbal reactions, speaking sentences that acknowledge bonds or that dissolve entanglements, and gestures that move towards healing, such as embracing. Family members who have been excluded are "discovered" and re-integrated into the family. Traumatic events are revealed in ways that diminish the effects of anxiety, isolation and a reduced capacity for love. Each and every member of the family must find an appropriate place in the system so that there is love and belonging, regardless of what has happened in the family.

There was a man in a group who was suffering from prostate cancer. The disease had led to many quarrels with his wife because they had different ideas of how he should deal with his illness. Their three children, ranging in age from six to ten, knew about their father's illness, but were not aware of how serious it was.

The man first set up a constellation of his present family in which he and his wife stood side by side, but at some distance from each other. The three children were placed relatively close together, facing their parents. When questioned, all the representatives reported feeling quite fine. The children were happy to be so close together, and felt loved and cared for by their parents. The man's wife, however, reported feeling a lack of warmth from her husband. In the second step, the therapist asked the man to add a representative for his illness. He chose a female representative and placed her very near his own representative, between his wife and himself. The new representative beamed at the man's representative and snuggled up to him. His wife spontaneously stepped a bit off to the side. When asked, she said that she found this situation incredible, and she felt annoyed and indignant. She said that if it weren't for the children, she would just take off. The man seemed not to even register her reaction, and reported; "Now I really feel good." The children took each other by the hand and moved backwards. The youngest child began to cry and dropped to her knees.

The therapist asked the man if he had been married or engaged prior to this relationship, but he said he had not. The therapist added representatives for the man's parents and placed them at his side, but at a distance. They looked at their son in a very friendly way, but the mother moved a bit farther away from her husband. The therapist asked the three children to stand with their mother and, together with her, move back until the youngest child felt able to stand up again. When the client's representative was asked for his reactions, he said that his attention was drawn to his parents, particularly his father, but the most important thing for him was that his illness remain near to him. The disease representative, however, reported a fundamental change in orientation. "My eyes are drawn to that man over there. I have lost the inner contact here where I am. I think I belong over there." She was asked to follow this impulse, and approached the man's father, pressing herself tightly against him. Then, she suddenly began to cry bitterly.

The therapist asked the client if his father had had a significant relationship with another woman before he married the client's mother. He recalled, "Yes, my father was engaged, but shortly before the wedding he met my mother. He broke off the engagement and married my mother, actually, on the same date that had been set for the wedding with other woman. Six months later, the previous fiancée committed suicide." The father's representative shook himself free of the disease representative's grasp, turned away and stood back to back with his wife, facing outwards. The representative of the illness fell to the floor and buried her face in her hands. She said quietly, but clearly audibly; "I am that fiancée!" She then lay on her back on the floor.

When asked about his feelings, the client's representative very cheerfully said he wanted to go and lie down with this woman. He did so and the two embraced warmly. The therapist asked the man's father if he wanted or was able to do anything for his son, but the answer was clearly, "No!" In the meantime, the man's mother had turned around to stand next to her husband. She also shook her head negatively in answer to the question of helping her son. (At the time of the constellation, both the client's parents were still living.) The therapist asked the disease/fiancée, but she wanted no contact with her former fiancé. The client's representative said that he needed nothing further; "I am fine here." The therapist ended the constellation at this point and asked the client if there was anything he felt he needed. He seemed quite light-hearted and said there was nothing more that he needed.

After the seminar, the man agreed to the treatment suggested by his doctors that he had previously refused. His willingness to undergo treatment greatly improved his relationship with his wife. Two years later, his condition suddenly deteriorated dramatically, and it turned out that the cancer had metastasized throughout his body. He came in for an individual session to get some support in preparing his children for his death. He seemed at peace with his fate.

One could rightly ask if there wasn't more that could have been done to release the bond between this man and his fatal illness, but that is very difficult to answer, and is beyond the scope of the constellation. The therapist uses the movements that emerge and the reactions of the client to follow the processes of uncovering and resolving. These processes are carried by the representatives in the course of the constellation and must be in harmony with the reality of the family system involved. Although the therapist can support the client and the representatives in finding resolutions, he or she cannot work against them, or against their feelings and reactions.

If a therapist were to push for a life-saving resolution, against the forces at the soul level of the constellation, and against the movements of the client, the most you could hope for would be a superficial resolution that would actually distract from reality. As therapist, you would quickly end up out of your depth and put yourself under enormous pressure in an attempt to be helpful. A side effect is a loss of the client's trust. In the constellation mentioned, the client's representative's wish to remain lying next to the "illness/fiancée" representative, clearly revealed a confrontation with death. This confrontation may have been a factor in the client's decision to undergo medical treatment. At the same time, his reaction made clear that, in his heart, he was basically in agreement with his desire or need to resolve something for his father through his own illness and death.

The purpose of a constellation is not to find a resolution "come what may"; it cannot make someone do something or convince them of anything that is not supported by the forces of the family system or the "greater soul". What a constellation has to say and how convincing it is arises out of the constellation itself. Sometimes a therapist may follow some image that the representatives would not have thought of, or the therapist might ask them to say or do something that they would have shrunk away from on their own. Often, this captures something essential for the client, something that can initiate movement. However, the therapist has to be prepared to check out such images, to make corrections when necessary, and to discard them when that is what is called for. Finally, the therapist has to fully trust the impact on the representatives and the client.

If the initial placement of representatives seems to support the family members in hiding important dynamics, it may be helpful to put their positions partially in order before asking for feedback or moving other family members around. Children are often placed in a way that covers up certain dynamics between the parents. If the couple's relationship is the foreground concern, the children can simply be moved out of their parents' relationship field and organised according to age on the edge of the constellation. This makes room for the couple's dynamics to take precedence.

All in all, it is better to go into more depth with a few family members than to try to meet everyone's interests completely. An attempt to fully capture the process of the soul, in all its complexity, is not only impossible, but it would rob the constellation of its power of resolution, its efficiency and orientation, and would diminish the potential for movement in the future. In an individual session the therapist has more freedom to investigate complex family dynamics.

It would be equally dangerous to try to press constellation processes and results into a logical structure, with cause and effect explanations. In the example above, we could not say that because the client's father failed to honour and respect his ex-fiancée and her suicide, his only son had to restore the connections with his own death. We can only sense that there is some connection, based on the images of the constellation. Our goal is not to provide explanations, but rather the kind of clarity that makes action possible. According to Werner Heisenberg, precision is the opposite of clarity.

So, a constellation should be clear, but not exact. It is not a portrayal of absolute truth, but nonetheless, some of the family's truth is present in a constellation. From a clarifying constellation, the client can easily take the grain of truth into his or her soul. When necessary, it can be adjusted to match the more exact internal and external details of the family's reality. Like a good painting, a constellation compresses reality, and certain distortions become meaningful. It may point to essential aspects more effectively than the actual family is able to do. It is not so much a question of "That's exactly how things are," as "that's it!" We are looking at a complete network of effects and interconnections, not at an analysis of reality based on causal relationships. The "whole" of a constellation is not reached through analysis, but through participation.

The Orders of Family Systems

We can differentiate between a new *internal* sense of order, or new orientation that is the result of spoken sentences of resolution or gestures between two people, and a new *external* orientation illustrated by a final, resolving image in which each and every family member in the constellation has found their rightful place and feels at ease in the system.

As constellation work has developed from the orders of relationships to include the larger movements of the soul in the context of illness, death, disaster and guilt, there is less emphasis on a resolving image for an entire family, one in which each member stands in their correct place. Constellations often end whenever some meaningful movement of the soul comes to light or whenever a healing process is discovered. In addition, constellations now tend to concentrate more on complex social relationship fields in which the orders of family relationships are insufficient to guide a constellation to resolution. For example, the injustices of the Nazi regime cannot be dealt with by finding a healing place in the family for each of their descendents.

Images of resolution in a spatially ordered family constellation are usually most meaningful when clients are trying to find a good place in their family. Common phrases such as: "There's no room in this relationship for...," "make some space for yourself," or "I'm in a good place" are formulations of experience that indicate that our relationships unfold within an experience of space and we need to make space and share space with others. A physical place cannot be occupied by more than one person. "Space" and "place" are fundamentally constant experiences of body and soul.

An older man in a group was having suicidal thoughts and he talked about guilt feelings that had plagued him for a long time. His eldest son had hanged himself in the attic following a row with his father (the client). In the interview, however, the son's suicide became clearer. This family of five children were living, crowded together, in a very small flat. Three days before the suicide, the boy's mother had announced at the dinner table that she was pregnant again. The eldest son jumped up in outrage and cried, "But we haven't got any room!"
The constellation was set up in an appropriate order by the therapist. The parents stood together facing their six children, who were arranged according to age from left to right. There were brief, moving dialogues between the father and his eldest son, and between the youngest son and his eldest brother who had made space for him. The sacrifice of the eldest child was acknowledged and accepted, and at the same time his place as eldest child in the family was affirmed, even beyond his death.

The experience of place and space in a family with many children is different from that in a small family. Also, there is a difference between knowing that you are the third child in your family, and the direct experience in a constellation of being placed in a row with your siblings, facing your parents and feeling the sensations. Siblings who died prematurely and were never really known, or have not been remembered, suddenly claim their place in a constellation and want to join the other children in the family. Relationships that never actually developed in physical reality, such as the connection to a father who was not actually known, feel suddenly within reach, experienced directly through their effects in the soul.

Sometimes there are very complicated family relationships, such as a woman client whose mother had had seven children from six different men. This woman did not really know her own father as an individual, but two of the other men helped raise all the children. Where is the right place for this woman to stand in her family? Another man was the only one of five children to survive a flu epidemic. How does he feel when he stands in a row of these five siblings and experiences body contact with them? What happens if you think you are the first and only child in a family and then find out one day that you have a sibling from a previous relationship of your father's? How does it feel to make contact with this brother or sister? How does an adopted child find the right place between biological parents and adoptive parents, and between biological siblings and adoptive siblings? How can a father find the right place in his family after spending five years in prison? How does a child find the right place in a family when the father had an extra-marital affair that resulted in a child who is between the third and fourth children in the family? Where is the best place for children in a family in which one of the parents has brought children from a previous relationship or marriage? What changes when such a couple have children together? Do aborted children have a place, and if so, with whom? Do they belong with their siblings, with both parents, or only with their mother or father? One of the primary fascinations with family constellation is due to the fact that they sometimes offer answers to such questions throug the images of a constellation, and through an actual physical sensation and awareness of the right place.

Finding a healthy family order in a constellation is the task of the therapist, as representatives cannot usually find their correct places on their own. They are entangled in the system just as the actual people they are representing. The therapist has the advantage of a basic knowledge of influential orders, confirmed by experience and an overview of the system based on observation from the outside. He or she needs feedback from the representatives, however, to confirm or deny positions. "Yes, this is good," or "No, I felt better over there, next to my mother."

A relationship system is "in order" when all representatives have found a place to stand that feels "right". The images of resolution in a constellation that are based on the orders of relationship may differ from one another, but the orders are not arbitrary. It may be that in a family where there has been a divorce, the siblings feel most comfortable when they are placed between their parents. In a different case, they might prefer to stand opposite their parents, but their parents feel best standing at some distance from one another. In another family, the children may all wish to stand near their mother or all opposite their father. At the end of a constellation, the position that most commonly feels good for children is standing in a row, according to age, facing their parents. This clearly separates the levels of parents and children, but allows them to maintain their connections. Parents can feel their responsibility towards their children, and the children can feel seen and "small", in the position of "taking". In the case of a family that is heavily encumbered in some fateful way, however, parents and children have sometimes felt best when allowed to all face the future together, hand in hand and to leave the difficulties behind them, at peace if possible. The most important factor is that an image of resolution be established that relieves and lessens the burdens, one that remains in memory, and that leads to resolving action. Then, it is probably "right".

Clarifying Images

An image of resolution occurs when appropriate movements and words lead to a configuration in which all the representatives and the client, either from within or without the constellation, feel comfortable and "right" in their places. In some constellations, there is a feeling like a sigh of relief and visible relaxation that runs through the entire family. Everyone's face looks open and clear, and sometimes radiant. I have heard from many clients that the image of resolution from their constellation continued to be a source of nourishment for them and in stressful situations later they found it supportive and helpful to be able to recall that image.

It would be foolish to expect that we can always arrive at an image of resolution that satisfies everyone. Often, the best we can hope for is a path that can shed new light on the bonds of fate and their consequences, or a constellation that moves to a decision point but leaves the actual ending open. Such decisions might include whether to separate from a partner, whether and when to bring a grieving process to a close, or even a decision whether to remain alive.

Although a good image of resolution is healing, it is sometimes advisable to refrain from completing a constellation "well" in this way. Particularly when there is some very difficult fate involved, there is greater strength available if the constellation is ended at the high point of the energy. That often brings more healing strength into the soul than a good image of resolution. In other cases, the images of resolution are not comfortable in the least, because they reveal consequences that are difficult to bear.

What does resolution mean? Do we really know exactly what is resolved? Does resolution always mean that there is a happy ending? Aren't there also resolutions that involve an acknowledgement that something is the way it is and cannot be changed, or that one has to face what is unavoidable, or to have faith in something that cannot be predicted or brought under control? Nonetheless, there must be something in the constellation process, as well as in the final image of resolution that in some way reflects what is "right" and will therefore continue working in the client.

Constellations are pictorial processes. Because relationships in the external world and our inner experiences are also structures in space, they are experienced and represented in visual terms. Conscious and unconscious visual representations are reflected in constellations through the representatives in a form that is visible from the outside, one that changes to reveal and guide as the representatives move and change positions. Accompanied by a new feeling quality, these images of resolution are taken into the internal "group" soul, where their influence unfolds. Some pictures, however, have to remain "external", namely those that involve negative burdens that have been taken on from another person, usually one's parents.

There was a woman who had already done a number of constellations about her difficulties in relationship to men. She had found clarity in many important areas of her life, but still had not managed to establish a long-term relationship with a man, nor had she come to terms with her mother. When she was with her mother, she often experienced her mother as distant and closed and she felt frightened by her in some way. The therapist first placed her mother in the constellation and asked her to follow any impulse she felt. After a while, in a trancelike state, she felt overcome by movements and sounds that were clearly sexual in nature and that expressed qualities of panic, fear, pain, aggression, shame, but also of desire. The therapist allowed the representative to continue with this powerful expression until she was exhausted. He then chose a representative for the mother's mother and led the mother's representative to be held in her arms. The mother closed her eyes and wept quietly to herself until she felt calm.

The client watched her mother's process, transfixed. At the end she said: "I have always suspected that my mother had some difficult sexual experience when she was very young. Thank you for making it possible for me to watch that for so long. What I saw is what I have always felt, but now it is out, and can remain with my mother. I feel like I can breathe freely for the first time in a long time."

A resolution like this, however, is often only an interim solution, useful but incomplete. In this case, the step that is still missing would be something to help re-open the connection to her mother without her feeling compelled to take on her terrible experience again. The family soul needs a process of resolution for the mother to let her experiences recede into a past that has been overcome. That can make loving contact between the woman and her mother possible again.

Statements of Bonding and Resolution

The "images" of a constellation often speak for themselves, and need no interpretation or explanation. Even when those outside the family might see various possible interpretations, the client is usually very clear, since he or she actually participates in the family system directly, and understands the situation at a soul level, even when it is hidden. Often, however, constellations only offer a sense of "rightness" and resolution once the hidden dynamics of the situation have been verbalised. The image brings awareness of the connections, and the words add resonance and strength. Sometimes the meaning of the representatives' movements only becomes clear through a brief description. Often the "movements of the soul" find direction and dynamics through an expression of "key sentences". I have cited examples of this phenomenon, for example, in some of the statements from the constellation of the Brazilian woman: "So many dead." "Won't anyone help me?" "I am so tired." In another constellation, the client's father was confronted with a representative who stood for "the flight from the homeland", and the father suddenly declared, "I have to shoot him, or I'll never get home." In yet another constellation, a woman representing the client pointed to her father's representative and stated with absolute certainty; "That is not my father!" Statements like these often actually do uncover unknown facts in the family, but this is just one function of verbalisation in a constellation. More frequently, words illustrate the bonds in a family and state what might provide resolution. Representatives or clients may be asked to repeat sentences provided by the therapist, making clear what is binding someone to the fate of another, or what might help to resolve and release the entangled connections. These sentences emerge from the constellation process and have a sense of rightness and release for the representatives. When a constellation is carried by the client's "group soul", such statements simply occur to the therapist or to representatives. They are words that touch and move the soul.

Articulating the dynamics of bonding serves to expose and clarify the existing bonds forged by fate. For example, someone might be asked to say, "Mummy, I will go to meet your sister in death, so you can remain here with Daddy." Or, "Dear Grandpa, you lost everything. I won't keep anything, either, and in that way I will remain close to you. If our family is critical of you, you won't be alone." These kinds of sentences often touch clients very deeply, because they express something that the person has somehow always felt, but never verbalised. In any such statement in a constellation, the family's situation is framed in the context of bonds of love.

Sentences of resolution serve to shift the effects of fateful bonds in the client's actual life. They do so by honouring the fate of those who are bound, and by acknowledging their pain and their love. They allow the consequences of fate to remain with those who have the responsibility and capacity to carry them alone. Usually, the consequences have already been suffered so the sentences of resolution do not change the facts, but only the effects. For example, the therapist might have a daughter tell her father's abandoned fiancée; "I see your anger and I understand your anger. I see the underlying pain, and I know this pain. In my own way I have lived a part of your life. Please remain friendly if I pull back now and move nearer to my mother, and if I leave behind anything that is unresolved between you and my father. For me, it was a blessing that my father married my mother and not you. Look with benevolence on the fact that I exist, even though I am not your child." It may be that only a short sentence is needed, for example, to a sibling; "You belong, just as I do." Or, perhaps one word is enough, for example, saying to one's father; "Thank you!"

Such sentences concisely express conflicts, communication, or loving bonds, and are aimed at the essential core of a relationship. They only hit the mark when they are spoken in an encounter between the people who are bound together

The therapist must remain alert to whether the representatives or clients are simply repeating words or whether they really can experience the statements as "on target", touching, and resolving. If the words do not ring true, the therapist needs to look for different sentences. If sentences of bonding and resolution do not lead anywhere, it often means that something else has to be resolved first between others in the system, or that there are critical dynamics that have not yet appeared. If it seems that the sentences are probably correct, but they don't move, or they cannot be taken in, then the therapist may have to return to the dynamics of the system. For example, a mother and father might need some appropriate exchange with each other before the client can face his or her parents directly. It might suffice to say merely, "You may have me as your child."

Sentences of bonding and resolution arise out of the "orders of love" and touch the core of constellation work. They express movements and orders in the soul, positive as well as negative, and they bring the images of the soul into harmony. Images demand words, as we know well from the vast quantity of literature available. Language that touches in a face-to-face encounter is eye opening. Our everyday experience of telephone calls that touch us and stir images in our soul gives us some measure of the psychotherapeutic significance of words, when they are focussed and connect to what is fundamental. The art of therapy is deciding how many and which words are needed.

Moving Rituals

In many constellations, visual and verbal experiences are complemented by ritual.

A ritual, a repeated, set procedure, binds a physical or physically supported gesture to the depths of reality. It allows the forces of the soul to be experienced physically, in a fullness that is not possible through verbalisation alone. The use of the word "ritual" here is perhaps not precisely correct, because constellations normally work with unique gestures that do not lend themselves to liturgical repetition. For many people, the word ritual is too religious. Since the beginning of the twentieth century, psychology and the behavioural sciences have secularised this word as an expression of standardised, typical, and habitual behavioural patterns. In constellation work, "ritual" means a relatively consistent procedure that may lead a client towards a healing, physical experience. In this context, I will look at two ritual processes, those of bowing down and of creating a line of ancestors.

Bowing Down

The German language has two different words for bowing, which indicate slightly different physical movements. This distinction seems useful in terms of family constellations.

In *"verbeugung"*, the client bows, commonly to the representative of a parent or parents, in a way that lessens an attitude of arrogance or presumption. This may be helpful when someone is refusing or unable to complete a reaching-out movement towards a parent, is acting in an arrogant manner towards a parent, has made serious allegations against a parent, or has physically attacked a parent. Presumption also includes situations in which children have been elevated above their parents out of feelings of love or an effort to help or rescue them. Bowing down lowers the children to a position of grown children who take and agree to what they have received from their parents. This restores a natural flow of life and love. It erases any temptation towards those feelings of superiority that destroy love. I have observed countless bowing down rituals that have helped clients let go of pent-up feelings of superiority and guilt that were originally born of necessity. Most of the time, parents are then able to turn to their children lovingly and respectfully in the constellation, and also in reality.

The word "lower" indicates a problematic aspect of bowing down in a constellation, and how delicately a therapist has to handle this ritual. Bowing down is not appropriate if the child feels humiliated by bowing, for example if it calls up memories of serious physical abuse from those parents. If a bow makes a person weaker, or means a loss of dignity, it is harmful. If a therapist is not certain whether a bow is a healing, helpful procedure or not, the reactions of the representatives usually provide reliable feedback about whether the movement has an appropriate and resolving effect. In addition, this allows the client the freedom to participate internally to an extent that he or she might feel shy about doing in front of others. A bow that is "right on," enhances the dignity of everyone involved. It strengthens, frees, and makes way for love to flow.

Many constellation leaders disagree about the usefulness of bowing down. It can be argued that it is more helpful to look behind the child's arrogance to discover the child's true love in the family system, and to uncover influential events and fateful connections so that the presumptuous attitude becomes superfluous and can be shed.

A bow often has a healing effect for the client's parents or grandparents, as well. It is clear that a therapist has no right to demand that a client's parents bow down before their parents or their fate, not even in a constellation, but through the use of representatives, we can look at what effects it might have on the system if these parents were able to bow down. If it proves to be possible in the constellation, it has probably already happened in reality and it may be that the client just has not really taken it in. In my experience, clients often feel supported and relieved when their parents have also bowed down and they also feel free to bow or simply to allow love to flow freely again. Despite the best of intentions, arrogance and presumptuousness hold potentially destructive consequences for clients and their families. This fact alone justifies the use of bowing down in constellation work. It is not a matter of chance that bowing has developed as a culturally significant ritual.

The second German word for bowing, "*verneigung*", has broader implications. This bowing down has less to do with one's own parents or personal arrogance, but rather with the influence of fate on a family and those who carry this fate. It is a larger expression of honour and respect, in which one bows down before those forces that lie beyond individuals and before the consequences of all those forces. We honour those of earlier generations for whatever belongs to them. We agree to the effects on our own lives that stem from the fate of others, and we allow that fate to find its final rest. A bow can mark the end of the past that frees the future of blockades and burdens.

This kind of bowing down is also only appropriate when it is done with respect and adds to the dignity of everyone involved. It is a movement that is made by adults. Children do not need to bow or to bow down, except as a cultural sign of respect, or in order to learn something that will be needed later. I once had an experience as representative of a twelve-year-old, in which I refused to follow the therapist's suggestion that I bow before my grandfather, who had been entangled in the Third Reich. I loved this grandfather, but bowing down to him, to his victims, and to fate was far too big a task for me. It would have been frightening and overwhelming for me to do so. I said that my feeling was that my Papa should bow down, but not me. I experienced a great sense of relief when I took my father's hand and snuggled up close to him, and saw how he bowed before his father and his father's victims. I didn't have to think about it at all, I could just look lovingly at my father, close to my grandfather, within the circle of his victims.

In addition to the movement of body and soul in bowing down, a significant component is straightening up again. It signifies courageous humility in the face of the reality of life, and the humble courage required to bear the human condition. It represents the strength to look another straight in the eye, to take on responsibility, to stand alone and with others, and a readiness to shoulder the weight of whatever one has to carry in life.

The Ritual of Standing in a Line of Ancestors

To tap into our life energy, it is useful to feel the strength of our ancestors and to be at home in our rightful place in the flow of life. In constellations, setting up a line of ancestors is a ritual that is a source of strength for descendents, but is also a way of getting feedback from representatives when there is missing information. Representatives may be able to pick up events that lie far back in the family history. A row of ancestors can be made up of couples, or might just be a line of male ancestors for a man or female ancestors for a woman. Particularly when a father and earlier males have not been experienced as a source of positive energy in reality, it can be very pleasurable for a man to stand in this line with his father, grandfather, great-grandfather, and perhaps even more generations behind him. Women who have been more connected to their fathers, or other men in the family, can find their way back to a source of strength in their mothers and other women in the family by standing in a female line of ancestors.

The line of ancestors can be taken in fully only when there is no interference between the person and his or her ancestors. If the line is interrupted and someone feels an urge to step out of the line or to step back, creating a gap, the therapist looks for information that might explain this interruption and, if possible, allow for correction. If there is no other information available, we have to rely on the reactions of the representatives and what comes directly from the constellation.

A woman in a couples' group was doing a constellation in connection with a sexual problem and she was set up facing her husband. Behind her husband was a long line of male ancestors and behind the woman was a long line of female ancestors. With the other men behind him, her husband reacted warmly towards his wife, with a lot of sexual energy. The client, however, remained stiff and untouched. Suddenly, the fifth woman in the ancestors' line fell down, as stiff as a board. (Luckily, the representative was not injured in this incident.) The client moved to the woman lying on the floor, looked at her curiously for a long time, and then walked over to her husband and embraced him warmly.

The client had no information that would explain this curious reaction, but the effects were immediately apparent and very powerful.

When parents have separated and their child has had limited or no experience of them as a couple, it may only be possible to set them up together behind the client after the child has been embraced by both parents, an embrace that may have been missing in reality. This is a ritual that reminds us that we receive life from both parents. The force of life that comes through our parents can be felt in their physical proximity and is reflected in deep, relaxed breathing.

In a line of ancestors, we can experience the sense of being held and carried by our parents, our clan, and the greater soul, and also gain an awareness of ourselves as adults and the strength that accompanies that recognition.

After the traumatic experiences and unresolved needs of the child have been worked through, and after a loving reaching-out movement, standing in a line of ancestors is a movement that brings stability, solidity, and strength. At the same time, this ritual opens a window to the future while the past, with all its positives and negatives, remains as a source of strength behind us and we can trust the forces that draw us forwards.

Constellations of the "Greater Soul"

In addition to family constellations, there are many other well-established forms of constellations. For example, there are structural constellations, organisational constellations, or political constellations. These have moved to concerns beyond a direct focus on the family soul, the parent-child relationships, family histories and their effects on the following generations. Although the main focus of constellations still lies in the area of psychological problems served by counselling centres, private counsellors and psychotherapists, interest has broadened to include the larger dimensions of the soul.

Our family relationships are also embedded in historical developments and larger, social networks of societal, cultural and political events. In Germany, for example, family events and their consequences cannot be isolated from the political events of the Third Reich, the Second World War, and sometimes even the First World War. Perhaps a mentally ill grandmother, or a Down's Syndrome great uncle was murdered in the euthanasia programme of the Nazis; a grandfather's Jewish fiancée disappeared into a concentration camp; property that came on the market at a low price because a Jewish family had fled became part of an Aryan family's inheritance; fathers who were doing their military service were killed in the war; fathers who to greater or lesser degrees participated in the murder of old people, women and children, or who were guilty of rape. Widespread conflict in the world, social injustice, human rights violations, and acts of terror, all point towards a need to look beyond family resolutions towards social processes that promote peace and reconciliation. Sometimes, when space and the size of the group allow, constellations can be used to address these larger issues. In constellations, representatives of Jewish victims have faced representatives of Nazi perpetrators, soldiers of enemy nations have stood facing one another, and representatives of revolutionaries have faced those of the government regime. The representatives were free to find their own movements, and to feel, through their experience in the constellation, what can bring peace to the heart in the context of such massive conflict and the broader dimensions of good and evil. Large political and social events take no notice of individuals or families but, nonetheless, individuals both cause and experience suffering. They are both, the "good" and the "evil", in an extremely complex network of effects. Family systems and larger systems are not only connected in neutral social interactions, but also through the love and hate of individuals.

Reconciliation is a major theme of the development of family constellations. We have repeatedly observed that whatever has been split off, excluded, and isolated strives towards a reunion to help us find peace within the reality of our personal, social, and "cosmic" life. This movement helps free our actions from victim-perpetrator entanglements, but when it cannot free us completely, it may allow us to at least be free of hate in our entanglements. To reach these goals, we very often have to look beyond a family structure. We can sometimes resolve something in the family soul, the focus of psychotherapy, when we are able to connect to the forces that also bring peace in the context of the greater soul.

A therapist looking at a client's difficult relationship to his father, for example, may choose not to put the client in the constellation at all. On the basis of the information given, the constellation might consist only of the client's father, who was a member of the SS Death's Head Division, and representatives for his fellow perpetrators and their victims. Or we might want to include the client's family and the comrades in battle who were killed when their tank exploded and the father in this family was the single survivor. It may become clear that the father was strongly drawn to his dead victims, or perhaps to his comrades who died in the war. Against the background of war and violent forces at work, an interrupted reaching-out movement between the client and his father appears in a very different light.

I would like to present two additional examples in which personal bonds are clearly embedded in larger networks and therefore demand constellations using the more open methods of the movements of the soul and a greater field of the soul.

A young woman, who was very attached to her father, was concerned about her failure in relationships with men. She described herself as too arrogant, and indeed she did seem rather proud, distant, and snobbish. It quickly became clear that her attachment to her father actually belonged to her beloved grandfather, her father's father. Her grandfather, Karl, had died when she was fourteen. An only child, this woman was named Karla. Her grandfather was a highly decorated general in the German air force and had participated in military planning. When many representatives, victims of bombardments, were lying on the floor and the grandfather was placed in front of them, he did not look at any of the dead, but raised his head and looked right over them. When he was asked to go to them and look at each one individually, he refused. It was clear that he could not do that. If he had had to look at the individuals who had lost their lives as a result of his military prowess, he would not have been able to do his work. When he was asked to lie down with the dead victims, the grandfather, at first, remained absolutely untouched. Only when he said aloud, "Now I will become dust just like you," did tears came to his eyes. When the client saw her beloved grandpa experiencing this pain, she too finally lowered her head, and tears came to her eyes.

The representatives of the victims, however, had no reaction. The events themselves were simply too anonymous. Just like her grandfather, the client could not really look at the dead victims. Who could, in such an enormous, terrible, and anonymous context? However, her grandfather's quiet tears in response to "becoming dust" helped the client to relinquish her attitude of superiority and she was able to move into her mother's arms. We do not know whether the constellation experience made any difference in her relationships with men, but she certainly was very different within the group, where she revealed her warm-hearted and loving side.

In a course in the United States, a woman wanted to look at her decision about whether she should return to Africa or not. She had been a development aid worker in a country torn by civil war, and she felt pulled to go back again. This was a career decision, not a family issue, but there was a family background in that her great-grandfather had been a landowner with many slaves. The therapist decided to do a large constellation, and chose representatives for the two sides of the civil war in this African country that had earlier lost so many to the American slave trade. He placed the two sets of representatives in two rows, facing each other. Then, he added two more sets of representatives for the European colonial powers, and for the American beneficiaries of the African slave trade. He placed these two groups facing each other on the other two sides, creating a closed square, with four rows of representatives. He put the client's representative in the row of Americans.

In a long process, in which the representatives were free to move according to their own impulses, very informative movements developed. The representatives of the two sides of the civil war engaged each other in a war-like way. In the course of this battle, some ended up lying dead on the floor. Most of the European colonists turned and looked away from what was happening. A few of the Americans also turned away, and others watched but did not move to get involved in the action. The client's representative, in contrast, tried to get between the battling enemies to separate them. Now and again, she bent down to the dead and appeared to be very agitated and impelled to action. Then something remarkable happened. First one, and then more, of the Africans from both sides of the war tried to get the client off the battlefield, as if they did not want her there. She fought her way back in, again and again, and was repeatedly pushed out.

The entire focus of action seemed to centre more and more on the development aid worker. For the outside observer, the terrible events in this country had disappeared and this woman stood in the centre. She became more and more desperate, but it appeared hopeless for her to stay with the Africans. Then, she found a gap and managed to get back into the circle, where she lay down with the dead on the floor. There, the others left her alone and returned to fighting each other. The therapist ended the constellation at this point.

The client had been watching the constellation attentively, and the therapist said to her at the end; "If you go back to Africa, watch out for your life." She had been in very life-threatening situations before, and now it was even clearer how dangerous it was for her. In addition, it had also become clear that help, or her kind of help, was not welcome. It was as if her urge to help stemmed more from her own needs than from the needs of the actual people there. Perhaps this woman was driven by some deep need to atone to her great-grandfather's slaves. Perhaps she needed to pay with her own life as recompense for her family's wealth that had been built on the backs of slaves.

The constellation was not discussed afterwards. The processes of the soul and the woman's decision had to remain free of any interpretation or explanation. Something had occurred in front of her eyes, an event the therapist knew nothing about, and had access to only through the constellation.

Constellations that take place in a relationship field that is greater than just one family, nonetheless remain connected to the reality of the family in the context of therapy and counselling. The bonds of love in a family system affect our soul's reactions to events and forces in the larger scene. The reality of our family and the larger reality that surrounds and contains it are interconnected in our souls. The family soul gives us our individual driving force, our images, and our aims and goals for resolution. The layers of the "greater soul" include what might be called spirituality and those energies that move beyond the family ties to resolution and release in acknowledging societal and religious realities. By religious, in this sense, I mean our connections to the larger, all-encompassing aspects of existence.

But, although we are all connected in these larger fields and systems as individuals and in relationship, these connections are not always of any practical value in solving our problems. Because constellations of these greater realms of the soul are often so impressive and moving for everyone involved, it is tempting for therapists to seek them out. If, however, that is not in accord with the issue at hand and not supported by the client's energy, the connection to the larger network of the soul will be insufficient to the task at hand. The connections remain general in nature, perhaps interesting, but without real meaning, and irrelevant to the action that is required.

Most constellations in a therapeutic or counselling setting remain focused on family structures. Symptoms or symbols that are set up in constellations frequently turn out to represent specific family members who have suffered. A war event that involved millions of people ends up, in a constellation, as meaningful in terms of the helplessness of one small child bound to a parent caught in the throes of war. Striving towards harmony with an all-inclusive reality, the movements of human or spiritual dimensions in a constellation always remain connected to the individual life energy, and to the flow of love towards a parent, a partner, siblings, children, or other closely related persons.

Ending a Constellation

The ideal point to end a family constellation is when resolution appears and the energy and strength are at their highest. The client can then leave the constellation charged with the energy of the resolution. The therapist has to feel a way into the process to find the point that marks the end of the constellation, one that is an appropriate beginning for the client that will support whatever comes next, or that will empower movement. Too many movements, or too much insight, often cover up what is really of essence. Too little allows the client to fall back into unknowing. Some constellations complete a developmental step, and some present new, surprising guidelines.

People are easily able to fill in those details that could overload a constellation or drag it down. If representatives are getting tired and there does not seem to be enough energy to carry the constellation to the next step, it is best to end it. If the client cannot take in any more, or the therapist doesn't have a feeling for the constellation, if things become confusing, or if there is no sign of binding and resolving love, the constellation has to be broken off or interrupted. There may be an opportunity later to start from a different point with more complete information, more openness to the process, more depth, or a greater sense of urgency and awareness of the underlying background.

Breaking off a constellation is often very painful for clients, but that pain sometimes prompts an interest in gathering more information about the family or might stimulate feelings and emotions that can be worked with more easily. It may help the client to differentiate between what is essential and what is not, and between what leads towards resolution and what distracts from it. If the constellation is not connecting to the reality of the family, the client will be content to break it off, because imagination and fantasy do not carry one very far.

No matter how brief the constellation, the client needs to have the feeling that what has happened is something that is important to him or her. The client naturally wants to feel heard, even if the therapist hasn't followed up on what the client initially wanted to talk about or if the constellation has led to something completely different from what was expected. The person understands that he or she is now alone with whatever the experience offered, and is solely responsible for carrying on with whatever has emerged. The end of the constellation ends the client's contact with the therapist. If there are problems that call for additional exploration, the client can initiate contact again, either during the seminar or at a later date.

Ending a constellation also means releasing the representatives, and some therapists use a ritual to achieve this purpose. For example, they might ask the client to take each representative by the hand, thank the person for their help, and explicitly release that person from the family field. Representatives normally move out of a constellation without any difficulty and immediately feel free of their roles. This is particularly true if the constellation has come to a resolution that is satisfying for all the representatives. We are not actually very vulnerable to the influences from the energy field of others.

Sometimes, however, there are representatives who continue to feel caught after a constellation has ended. Some roles demand more involvement and empathy on the part of the representatives and they cannot be so easily shrugged off from one moment to the next, particularly if there was a difficult issue that has not been neatly resolved. It may help for the representative to mentally look at the real family member and say; "I will stay with you and your difficult fate for a while and honour you by doing so. Then, I will withdraw." Usually, within a short period of time the representative feels free of the role and any effects.

We do not have to worry unduly about representatives, even when they are subjected to heavy burdens in constellations. Now and again, there is a risk of temporary physical symptoms, or even mental symptoms resembling psychoses, but people can almost always sense clearly what belongs to the role and separate it from what belongs to them, personally. If a particular person feels overwhelmed by a role, he or she must be removed from that role. The therapist has to be skilled at handling such extreme situations. It might be useful to ask the person a completely unexpected question that orientates everyone to reality again, or do something that suppresses hyperventilation, or make firm physical contact that allows for no resistance. I have rarely needed to take such measures, and have seldom seen representatives continue to suffer effects from a role over any length of time after they returned home. In such cases, it usually turns out that the role was an impetus that released something in the person's own family that was in need of resolution.

The therapist also releases the client from the engagement and the therapist is then empty and ready for another client. The more resolution and resonance there is at the end of a constellation, the easier it is for the therapist to move on. If he or she has a feeling that a constellation was unsuccessful, it sometimes requires a strong act of will to let go of the constellation and that client. If there is a sudden "hindsight" image, the therapist might offer the client a visualisation, a short exercise, or a short constellation from a different viewpoint.

It takes practice to resist more intervention than is absolutely necessary for the client and the constellation, and to let the client go again. Other skills that are invaluable for the therapist include staying open to mistakes and recognising the errors without becoming weighed down by them, or getting caught up in regrets. If these things are difficult, it generally means that the therapist has slipped into a transference/ counter-transference process with the client, in which both of them are trying to hold on to the relationship as if it were a parent-child relationship. A therapist can also get trapped by personal, unresolved issues, such as a childish helplessness in the face of parental needs, and an accompanying desire to be all-powerful and helpful.

Most of the time, though, constellations are beneficial for therapists, as well as the client, the representatives and observers. It is an opportunity to briefly participate in a wide variety of human fates, always in a way that is respectful towards everyone, with a trust in life, and in the service of resolution.

5 Applications and Effects of Family Constellations

Constellation work has developed into a kind of general, all-purpose method for setting up configurations of systemic processes in all human relationships. Almost every aspect of soul relationship can be set up in a constellation: all kinds of human relationships, the internal connections of body, mind, and soul in one individual, and other internal and external processes, including connections in material, social and spiritual realms. To what extent this is appropriate, useful, or conducive to the future development of constellation work is still an open question. At present, we can confirm that, in addition to family constellations, constellations of structural "parts" and constellations of relationship dynamics in teams, organisations, and even extending into political areas have already proven of value. There are also various experimental areas where interesting issues warrant further exploration.

Family constellations, however, are concerned with the soul field of the family, including representations of more abstract phenomena such as illness or a country, and they are meant to serve the process of resolution in families. The following discussion of applications and effects is to be understood solely in this context.

The Setting: Group, Individual, Telephone Sessions

The method of family constellations was originally developed in group therapy and personal awareness groups. The therapist in this approach, however, is not looking at group dynamics. That is, he or she is not working with relationships and interaction of group participants, and is not focussing on the social behaviour of participants with others in the group, nor is anyone's constellation discussed with the group. Structurally, constellation work is individual therapy in a group context, using the "resonating body" of the whole group, and inviting group participants to take part in others' constellations as representatives. The therapist approaches clients' problems through constellations rather than constructing them out of a group process. From the start, it is not the inner dynamics of a client and that person's behaviour that are in the foreground, but the relationship system, as it is carried in the individual's soul. We could speak of it as individual therapy with focus on the system, taking place within a group.

Since most people looking for help with emotional problems turn to individual therapy (or couple, or family therapy), a need quickly arose for some way to adapt the constellation approach to these settings in private practice, clinics, or counselling centres. Accordingly, new methods have been developed that allow this work to be done individually. As a substitute for a group, the therapist may provide shoes, cushions, sheets of paper, or various types of figures to represent or mark the positions in the client's relationship system. Setting up a constellation in this way allows an externalised picture of the relationship system, a "dissociated" observation from various positions (for example, the client looks at figures on a table from outside the system), or an "associated" sensory experience (the client, for example, can physically move from one floor marker to another, feeling the difference in various family positions). The therapist uses his or her observations, feelings, and awareness in place of actual representatives to enable the client to experience the bonds and resolution in the processes of the soul described in Chapter 3.

In individual work, there is not much that is essentially different from a constellation experience in a group in terms of resolution and a sense of being touched. What connects the methods is an unfolding in a spatial dimension, visualisation, an experiential focus on soul processes and the surprising and moving experience of the "knowing field", the therapist (optimally one with group experience), and the client's insight. Even in a telephone session, questions from the therapist and a guided imagination may prove helpful for a client. Here, too, what is critical is locating the events and fates in a family that are crucial to a resolution, and a visualisation or image of relationship experiences. Imagination is a spatial experience of "images". Experiences in the soul are, by their very nature, spatial experiences.

The advantage of doing constellations in a group lies primarily in the fullness of the experience for each participant, through the confrontation with many different fates, and the opportunity for a variety of experiences as a representative. During the final round in a group, it is not uncommon for people to make comments to the effect that, although their own constellation was a good experience, they learned even more from being representatives in various roles. (De Philipp, 2006).

Applications

Because constellations can be used to represent any human relationship, the applications are widespread. They can overcome obstacles to development and growth in an individual personality. They can help someone make peace with a complicated family history. They clarify, deepen, and ease relationships between parents and their children, between couples, between grown children and their parents (alive or deceased), and between siblings or other family members. They can include career and professional issues or pending decisions. With respect for the client and a focus on potentially relieving effects, constellations can address the connections between family events and illness, negative behavioural symptoms such as anxiety, compulsions, addictions, or psychotic behaviour. They provide an orientation for looking at behaviour in adoptive and foster families as well as non-family social settings such as homes or institutions. They can be used in training and supervision, and extend to use in schools, organisations, businesses, and broader social fields. But, there is always a central focus; where is a client and his or her problem connected to the fates of others? What are the relationship dynamics, beyond time and space that must come to light to allow the social reality to be shaped in a good way? Which orders of relationship allow life to thrive? A family constellation that provides answers to such questions is clearly a good experience for many people. But, do they help in a deep and on-going way?

The Results of Family Constellations

So far, there have been very few scientific studies to document the positive effects of family constellations (Höppner, 2001), and it is still unclear how many papers and dissertations are currently being written on constellation work worldwide. At this point, we are dependent upon the personal impressions of many therapists, on verbal and written feedback from participants, and the fact that clients very frequently recommend the method to others.

When we take this input into account, it would appear that constellations have a good effect, particularly in the areas of resolving couple and family conflicts, positively influencing behavioural difficulties with children, helping with problems in school, work, and decision-making, ending quarrels with parents, finding a sense of peace in one's soul and in one's family, lowering the risk of suicide and accidents, and in generally strengthening and supporting a basic life energy.

There have also been reports of improvement in some cases of illness and with some diseases (such as neurodermatitis), and of relief from symptoms such as anxiety or eating disorders. Children's difficulties seem more amenable to improvement than adults' problems, particularly when an adult life pattern or somatic process has already been set. There are fewer indications of healing effects in cases of severe depression or acute psychosis. One factor, of course, is that people who are very ill do not, as a rule, undertake to participate in a constellation group on their own, and the work is not yet widely known in psychiatric clinics and institutions. Surprisingly, however, many doctors and alternative healers are sending their patients for constellation work when they have the impression that the health problem in question is somehow connected to relationship difficulties or some blow of fate suffered by the family. Family constellations are not intended to cure diseases; they can, however, resolve attendant conflicts in the soul, thus making it easier for clients, doctors, and psychiatrists to deal with illness and symptoms. Serious trauma, particularly in an acute state, usually calls for more specific intervention than that offered by constellation work. Addicts who are actively dependent usually need medical attention and social supports, such as Alcoholics Anonymous, but a constellation may have a relieving effect on the emotional background. Deficits in learning that are due to socialisation require support over an extended period of time, and anyone interested in exploring and changing personality structures also needs to seek out a more appropriate therapeutic or spiritual setting.

Constellations are always concerned with the connections between symptoms and relationship dynamics. For example, we often see addictive behaviour in families in which the father is missing, or cannot offer support and strength to his children. The mother of the family then, directly or indirectly, communicates the message that what is good in life is only available from Mother, not from Father. In the case of young girls suffering from anorexia, the dynamics often seem to involve the child's resolve to disappear rather than allowing her father (sometimes her mother) to go, particularly when the girl feels a parent's pull towards death. Children suffering from neurodermatitis frequently seem to come from families in which a previous partner of the mother or father has been excluded and there are accompanying negative feelings.

Such examples, however, have not yet been scientifically investigated and documented. They may be useful for clients and therapists in forming a working hypothesis and orientation in the search for resolution, as long as everyone remains open to other, alternative connections in the soul. Many constellation leaders, and of course clients as well, would prefer to be able to clearly identify the connections between systemic dynamics and symptoms, and this could be an interesting field for future research. Up to now, however, we can only say that certain emotional or systemic conflicts seem to have various effects on symptoms and we cannot identify exact cause-and-effect processes. The word "symptom" is an indication that certain mind-body manifestations are a result of multiple factors, including chance, that have jointly produced these effects. Genetic disposition, learned behaviour, painful personal experiences, the family history, and broader social issues combine in their effects to a greater or lesser degree, and are all subject to accidental circumstances. A wide variety of therapeutic approaches might be possible and/or necessary to foster healing and resolution. Often, healing and change occur simply because a particular intervention does not allow a structure to continue as before and it collapses. The end effects reveal which methods are most appropriate for achieving particular results.

The question in family constellations is often: "In what context would these symptoms make sense?" Rather amazingly, family constellations unearth the "sense" of symptoms in actual occurrences in the family history, often even when the client had no direct involvement. A psychiatrist in a group once called symptoms "the last-minute panic" of a system. They force unresolved family issues to come to the surface and push for resolution before they have been forgotten or it is too late. Modes of behaviour, illnesses, and statements that are incomprehensible in terms of a client's actual life, often reflect, with astounding accuracy, what happened earlier to someone else in the family.

There was a man who was convinced that the Mafia was after him. One day, in the grip of his delusion, he stabbed a stranger on the street. The victim, an old man, was seriously, but not fatally, injured. The delusional man was confined to a psychiatric institution. In an effort to understand what had happened to her husband, the man's wife did some research into his family's history. What she discovered was that his paternal grand-father had been a wealthy farmer, a Mafioso according to village rumours, who had acquired a large part of his property through very questionable business dealings. In addition, the daughter of a small farmer from a neighbouring village got pregnant by this man, but he denied paternity of the child. The young woman, who lived in poverty with her mother, committed suicide at the age of twenty. When the grandson's wife learned of this family background, she felt a sense of relief because her husband's delusion and his actions finally made sense, albeit bitter, in terms of some kind of delayed balance of fate.

When such connections come to light with sufficient clarity, it can bring immediate relief and healing. In the example above, this was at least true for the man's wife and children. Of course, we can always find some "sense" of a matter if we look long enough and intensively enough. There are fates in every family that will somehow "match up". But, not every connection or just any "sense" will help. The most important criteria are that the "sense" makes sense, that it is experienced as "right on", and above all that it has the effect of resolution.

Sometimes it may prove worthwhile for a client to persevere through many constellations looking for a systemic solution to some particular problem. As with any other methodological convictions, however, it is sometimes tempting to look at a constellation that does not provide resolution and say, "We just haven't yet found the critical family problem," instead of helping the client in some other way or suggesting a different therapeutic approach. A therapist needs sensitiv-ity and practical experience to handle such situations well.

It is not a simple matter to set up a precise, scientific investigation into the effects of family constellations. The same could be said, of course, of all psychosocial areas of study. Questionnaires and statistical research are frequently too vulnerable to interpretation and are often most useful in situations where behaviour can be precisely analysed and operationalised. In the context of complex human problems, each with its own unique fate, it is difficult to compare one with another, or to apply such techniques.

Constellation work presents an additional obstacle in that constel-lations reflect systemic effects over many generations, past, present and future. Checking the facts is often impossible, and proving cause and effect relationships over such an extensive time frame is hardly imaginable. If a constellation is analysed down to the last detail, we lose the fundamental basis of the work, namely, the processes in the soul, the inclusive sense of "more than", in contrast to the scientific interest in exclusivity, "nothing other than". Phenomenological methods are the only tools we have for providing a sense of the complex totality of an event and its effects. It is similar to Chinese characters; they cannot be analysed simply according to the lines and marks, but require an awareness of the entire picture in order to grasp the meaning. Finally, we cannot work out the meaning of a family constellation in terms of linear cause and effect connections, because constellations consist of primarily pictorial and condensed processes. Research into effects to prove causal relationships would probably be a futile endeavour. Systemic complexities in the soul can be comprehended through pictures and images, by disruptions or changes in patterns, and in insights based on experience, but not through explanations and proof.

The Effects of a Family Constellation

We can hope that scientific interest is growing in constellation methods and its applications, but regardless of scientific involvement, therapists are called upon to work with constellations in a competent, well-grounded way, to concentrate on precise observation and awareness and to aim for the best possible effects from a constellation.

The first measure of the effect of a family constellation is the immediate, direct experience of the client, the therapist, the representatives, and the whole group. This must confirm that the process is making sense, easing the situation, and providing strength and support. This can be observed in many physical reactions, for example, a change in breathing patterns, a change of facial expression, or a verbal reaction. The "rightness" of the constellation can be felt in the "aha" experience of the whole group as well as the general atmosphere. A group will react very sensitively to the "truth" of a constellation as the feelings flow into the group. One of the advantages of constellation work is that it is not dependent upon the reactions of only the client and the therapist, but can be checked out in the reactions of the representatives and the effects on the whole group. One of the few real mistakes a therapist can make in the constellation work is to overlook the palpable effects of single steps within the constellation or of the constellation as a whole. A constellation will fail if it is "done" by the therapist over the client's head and heedless of the strength and receptiveness of the person that has to carry it.

In any event, I have experienced many constellations that looked very "complete", and which the representatives, therapist and the whole group all felt good about, but that had no real effect on the client or the client's problem. I have also experienced constellations that seemed very heavy and oppressive, with no positive resonance of feelings, that were regarded as worthless, or a failure, but nonetheless had a very clear impact and prompted changes in the client's life. We can remain tuned in to our awareness but, in the end, the effects of a constellation extend far beyond this. A constellation may initiate a helpful movement for the client, but it grasps only the tip of what is happening in the family system and in the soul. It would be difficult to predict what effects a constellation might have on someone's life. When it comes down to it, the complexities of the soul and the influence of necessity, chance, and freedom are beyond our comprehension.

That said, it is still amazing how often the reactions of representatives accurately anticipate later effects of a constellation. In one constellation, a woman had an intense, open encounter with her father, and reported the next day that her father had phoned her the previous evening after the constellation, for the first time in twenty years, and he chatted with her for a long time in a very friendly way. Or, during a constellation done by a married couple, the representative of their schizophrenic son felt great relief, but the representative of the anorectic daughter remained confused. The same effects then appeared in the family in reality. A woman had been waging a legal battle with her ex-husband about alimony for the previous ten years. Through her constellation, she reached a new understanding of the underlying factors in their divorce and was able to look at her ex-husband with appreciation at a level that did not get caught up in the issue of blame. A few days later, her ex-husband called her, invited her out to dinner, and the two of them settled the financial situation in an amicable way, without any need for lawyers. A man discovered a previously unknown sister in the course of a constellation. When he actually met this sister in reality, their meeting mirrored the warmth of the meeting in the constellation, even down to their gestures.

Connections to The Facts

Many times, constellations work from indications that stem from the representatives' reactions. There may be a powerful impact from the movements of the representatives without any clarity about the actual family background, perhaps because that information is not available. Sometimes, such constellations have a very beneficial effect, but a long-lasting, helpful change is more usually supported by the emergence of relevant information after the constellation. When someone feels bad after their constellation, which does happen, it is usually because the client is burdened or constrained by a lack of clarity, a sense of doubt, or by erroneous assumptions. Concrete information normally helps in such a situation. Facts help to clarify and make the constellation comprehensible, or provide a basis for revising the person's understanding of what was meant.

There was a young, very attractive therapist in an advanced training course. She wanted to set up a constellation because she was suffering from a rare autoimmune disease. She had a boyfriend, but couldn't have sex with him because it always resulted in a vaginal infection. She was first asked to set up representatives for herself and her boyfriend. She placed the two as if they had nothing to do with one another. The boyfriend's representative was taken out of the constellation and the woman chose two additional representatives, one for her vaginal infections and one for her autoimmune disease. She chose a woman for the first symptom, and a man for the disease and placed them in relation to her own representative. The representatives were then allowed to follow their own impulses and movements. The representative of the vaginal infection pulled the woman's representative to the floor and held her firmly there. Finally she held the woman in her lap, like a very small child. The "disease" marched back and forth like a soldier. The actual woman, who was watching the constellation from the outside, was very moved and began to weep. She could feel the "loving attraction' of the physical symptom that drew her down to the floor.

When she was asked if the constellation was understandable for her, she said; "It is connected to me but I don't know how." She had no information about events in her family that made any sense of what happened in the constellation, but she still appeared to experience some relief. As the seminar continued, however, she felt worse and worse, and talking to her during the breaks did not help. Two months later she wrote a letter reporting that she was doing so poorly that she didn't really know what to do and was considering dropping out of the training course. The therapist suggested that she gather some information about her family history. She went to visit her now aged father (her mother had already died) and asked what had happened in their family. She discovered that when her father was a young soldier, on three separate occasions he was the sole survivor of his entire group. Once, he was on watch duty and was unable to warn his troops of an impending attack, and was only able to save himself. This could have been a possible explanation for the soldierly movement in the constellation.

The second bit of information that she received was that her grand-mother, her father's mother, had to provide housing for an English officer at the end of the war. She had a relationship with him and got pregnant. No one knew what had happened to the child. The young woman could also now understand what had happened in the constellation when the "symptom" pulled her to the floor and held her like a little child. Her fateful connections to her father and her grandmother were clearly vis-ible. The young therapist felt very energised when she had incorporated this new information. She finished her training course and now leads constellations herself.

How Clients Deal With a Constellation

After a constellation, a client should be left in peace to have enough time to allow the experience to have its effect. Family constellation work has sometimes been criticised because the experiences of a constella-tion are not discussed or analyzed with clients or with the group. We must ask, though, what the impact of a discussion or analysis would be. The information content of the constellation might be more pre-cise, but less holistic as a consequence. The effects of images would be sacrificed in exchange for explanations. People might feel the need to justify their reactions or awareness, but with no chance of retriev-ing the actual events of the constellation. It is more likely that such an analysis would allow the client less inner freedom to let the constella-tion have an effect in an appropriate, truly personal form.

Having an experience and talking about an experience are not the same. Explanation is smaller and less effective than insight. One might describe a family constellation as a hypnotherapy process for the group soul. Conscious and unconscious processes work together, in a differentiated way, compressed in the experience of the constella-tion process. The definitive criteria for the "rightness" of a constella-tion is not whether it can be explained or not, but rather the degree of strength, relief, and clarity that the constellation awakens in the client. These effects may not be apparent immediately following a constella-tion, but often appear some time later.

Although constellation work is a brief therapy method, solutions seldom crystallise immediately. A constellation lasts for about 30 minutes, but the effects on the client's daily life only become apparent gradually. One man wrote, five years after participating in a group, "Now I understand. Thank you." A woman who was seriously ill with cancer was unable to accept the picture in her constellation that death was standing lovingly near her. She wrote, a year after the course, "I battled against death for a long time. Then, I accepted him at my side and I am living." When the therapist or the constellation confronts someone with things that are difficult or unpleasant to take in, this approach leaves the person free to deal with it whatever way is personally appropriate.

After a constellation, clients often ask if they should take some concrete action. Should a partner, parents or children be told? Is it a good idea to seek out this unknown half-brother? Usually the answer is: "Wait. When the process is ripe in your own soul, you will recognise the right time and the right situation to do or not do something." It is similar to the Taoist teaching of non-doing.

The therapist might suggest that a client do something or another, to emphasise what the constellation has revealed. The client must understand, however (and in certain circumstances may need to be reminded), that he or she is responsible for any actions or reactions. The therapist does not normally check on what a client does after a constellation, and, in fact, withdraws from the actual implementation of solutions. Most people value the degree of independence and self-reliance offered in constellation work, and feel the respect accorded their own responsibility.

However, it is also true that sometimes a client cannot come to terms with the experience or results of a constellation and continues to feel bad afterwards. Sometimes there is new information about the family history and the person does not know what to do with it. The constellation may have resolved the outer layer of a problem, baring the next layer in the soul, or new problems have arisen, or old problems have returned in a new form. In such cases, the therapist has to be available; either by phone or by letter, for an individual session or participation in another group, or to provide a recommendation for another kind of help elsewhere. A repetition, or reworking, is not what is called for in such cases, but the next step. It may be appropriate for a client to do another constellation after a period of time, but it is always a new, unique process that focuses on a new situation at a different time.

6 Comments on a Theory of Family Constellations

At this point in time, there is no complete theory of family constellations. Bert Hellinger has worked very practically, focussing on the relationship problems of people in need who come to him for help. Schooled in philosophy and theology, and steeped in spiritual practice, he has moved a long way from pastoral counselling and education, through various approaches including group dynamics, psychoanalysis, primal therapy, family therapy, and transactional analysis. He has entered into and explored many new methods as they have appeared on the scene, including Milton Erickson's hypnotherapy, NLP, and various approaches to relationship systems utilising "role players". Although aware of the various theoretical formulations, Hellinger has always been more interested in the effects of a method. He has continued to integrate, simplify, compact, and incorporate whatever seems appropriate and helpful for resolution in the soul, and to leave out what was inappropriate or not helpful. His adaptations have taken on his own form and his own personal style, becoming something of his own. In the end, he always relies on his own systemic awareness and his sensitivity to effects. He is not a man of science and academia and, although he was previously a Catholic priest, he has never seen himself as a representative of an institution. He has had very little personal interest in scientifically investigating what he does, or in founding any "school".

But he has explained and generalised some of the insights and ideas that have emerged out of the practical work, or in connection with this work. In this sense, of course, family constellation work has at least implicit theoretical elements. Also, to the extent that other psychotherapists and counsellors take over family constellation methods and integrate this approach into their own practice and world view, the methods and fundamentals will naturally be reflected in those applications. If family constellation work proves helpful as an independent method over a longer period of time, then the theoretical considerations will also deepen. This could provide an impetus for new, effective improvements in the practice, and reciprocally, also enrich our capacity for experiencing the processes of the soul and of human relationships.

The term "theory" stems from ancient Greek and originally referred to "looking at God", which was actually how the audiences in the theatre experienced it. It was then expanded to include any "looking" that had to do with connections in the mind. In our present view, "theory" generally means any systematic summary and generalisation of knowledge that explains reality. In our narrow sense, we associate theory with a need to verify assertions experimentally and with the potential for prediction.

As is true of most sociological and psychological theories, the theoretical elements of family constellations arise from generalisations drawn from experience, or from general assumptions that can only be tested in constellation experiences. There have been few opportunities for controlled, experimental classification or any extensive consideration of how that might be practical and meaningful. If anything there has been a reluctance to think in terms of research that would quantify the effects, for fear that it would dilute the uniqueness of the constellation experience and interfere with the clients' process of personal implementation.

At this point, a theory of family constellation work is most identifiable through what has been said about conscience and the conscious and unconscious processes of bonding and resolution. We might speak of a systemic theory of bonding. Additionally, questions about the interaction and effects of personal and systemic trauma are finding some initial answers (Ruppert, 2005), and there is currently much discussion of the theoretical issues of phenomenology and constructivism, more simply said, how much of the systemic "truth" of a constellation comes from the constellation itself, as opposed to being constructed by us.

I will address some general questions about the phenomenal of representatives' experiences in family constellations, about constellations as a phenomenological and systemic method, about the issue of "helping", and the position of family constellation work in psychotherapy, life assistance and practical philosophy. What I am venturing to say is preliminary at this stage, but may contribute to the discussion about family constellations. I am convinced that our basic understanding of the processes of the soul can be significantly broadened both by the experiences of constellations, and also the tentative conclusions and questions that arise out of this experience.

Representatives' Awareness

What allows representatives to mirror the words, gestures, feelings, behaviour and symptoms of total strangers with such surprising accuracy in constellations? Unfortunately, there has been little documentation aside from what we can see in the videos and read in the case studies in the books by Bert Hellinger and others. Meanwhile, however, the accumulation of experiences has grown immensely. The question remains how precisely these representation processes have been observed and how they can be explained.

The term "knowing field", coined by Albrecht Mahr, has become the name for a phenomenon that occurs in constellations, but what does it really mean?

Model of Explanation

In examining representative sensory awareness, any scientific observation will surely turn first to methodical analysis. We can compare the facts provided by the client with the accompanying reactions of the representatives. In many constellations, however, the representatives have no information, either because no facts were collected before the constellation, or because the client simply has no information. In addition, in our experience, most representatives do not seem to be particularly influenced by prior information, but rather unerringly follow what it is that they experience in the constellation field.

We might attempt to examine and check out the slightest, subtlest gestures and expressions, both verbal and non-verbal, of the client and also of the therapist, and note whether the representatives are picking up on these cues. This could explain some of the surprising reactions of the representatives. Representative awareness in constellations also touches on the more basic question of the process of awareness in families. How is information passed from one generation to the next? Besides conscious communication, there are certainly subliminal paths of information transfer. Theories of communication and behaviour, descriptions of hypnosis processes, and examinations of the interaction between mother and child in the research on bonding, all try to explain how and through what channels unconscious and preconscious information is passed from person to person, and how it is received and processed. These theories may suffice for an understanding of family dynamics and processes over generations, but do they also explain the puzzling phenomenon of representative awareness? And, the other way round, isn't the kind of awareness that we observe in the reactions of representatives actually what first happened in the actual families? Can we not suggest that the experience of representative awareness offers a new understanding of how we participate in the awareness and knowledge contained in our relationship network?

We can assume that the spatial structure of a constellation implicitly calls upon stored knowledge in the representative's brain, whether genetic in origin or learned. We all know intuitively, confirmed in the meantime by scientific experiments (Schlöter, 2005), that in a group setting, certain positions and movements can prompt particular feelings and thoughts that most people in the group will experience and understand in similar ways. Still, we can see that almost identical configurations in constellations often produce reactions in the representatives that differ widely from case to case, and are sometimes very unexpected. How can we explain the fact that a representative of a child placed in front of his or her parents, leaning back against them, in one case will turn and fall weeping into the parents' arms, and in another case will move away towards a window, or get terrible cramps and fall down? And how can we explain the fact that these processes mirror the actual processes in the real family? What has been added to the spatial experience to make a representative of a grandfather feel like a hanged person, although he knew nothing about the grandfather's suicide by hanging, and perhaps the client himself learned of the facts only after the constellation was finished?

In constellation circles, the ideas of the biologist Rupert Sheldrake, and his research into morphic fields, is often cited as one possible explanation. Sheldrake purports the existence of morphic fields, guiding forces in systems that are reflected in patterns and structures of otherwise random and coincidental processes. Through the influence of attractors, systems are drawn towards end points in the future. The field would have a history that contains, through the process of morphic resonance, an inherent memory that affects the present from the past, independent of the constraints of time and space. In systems organised by such fields, all parts are integrated with one another, through the field of the entire system. All mental activities have a strong connection to the brain, but attention and intention reach out much further. Sheldrake has postulated a "mind" function in biological fields that extends beyond the activities of the brain, and is accessible through a "sixth sense".

In any case, no one actually knows what morphic field are or how they work, and an explanation using known physical fields is probably not possible. We may have to assume the existence of some new field that has not yet been discovered or explored by physicists. There have been physicists who have proposed the existence of such fields. Ervin Laszlo, a musician and self-taught physicist, has described a "fifth field" or "psi-field". The existence of such a field could explain connections between spirit and cosmos, matter and consciousness, and also connect some ancient esoteric teachings and the great religions with a new understanding of natural sciences. Laszlo is suggesting that if events and objects existing separately in the universe are actually interconnected, we can make certain assumptions. The atoms of a given system of coordinates are able to reciprocally recognise their individual states. The genomes of living organisms are capable of adjusting to relevant aspects of their environment. Human brains and consciousness are able to communicate with each other in a transpersonal way, beyond the restrictions of space and time. (Laszlo, 2002)

Similarly, the journalist Lynne McTaggart (2003), having done extensive research in the world of physics, proposed the existence of a "zero-point field". She suggests that the findings of modern physics, primarily quantum theory, imply the existence of a universal and limitless sea of energy in which we are all interconnected with one other and with the world. Through quantum information processes that simultaneously pulsate through our mind and body, we can be in resonance with the entire world. Our human awareness would then be complete, due to the reciprocal effects of subatomic particles in the brain and this vast sea of quantum energy. This would propose a plausible explanation for hitherto inexplicable phenomena such as mind reading or communication at a cellular level, even what C. G. Jung called the "collective unconscious". McTaggart's findings also support Sheldrake's morphogenetic field theory.

It appears that quantum physics not only has the potential to change our image of physical reality in the cosmos and the subatomic world, but also offers a completely different model of reality that moves towards a new understanding of the processes of mind and soul. Natural science and the humanities might have a common basis of understanding through holistic thinking, where experiences from religion and spirituality as well as peculiar phenomena such as mind reading or premonition could be related to our current knowledge in traditional natural sciences.

The esoteric theories of a mainstream physicist, Anton Zeilinger, stem directly from quantum physics research and come to the conclusion that "information is the fundamental component of the universe", and "reality and information are the same thing" (Zeilinger, 2003). Zeilinger was of the opinion that "we should find a new term that contains both, reality and information. We can see a conceptual problem here, because there is no such term and it is clearly difficult for us to even think of such a concept." (Zeilinger, 2003)

He turned to philosophy for assistance. As a lay person in the fields of natural science and philosophy, it is somewhat daring of me to presume to use the word "soul" for such an elusive concept, as in the description in Chapter 3, since this is a word already heavily laden with old meanings at multiple layers. But even in ancient Greece, Aristotle was trying to bring together the monistic materialism of Democritus and the dualistic concepts that attribute soul with a non-material existence, independent of the physical body. He attempted to describe the soul as a principle of form and effect, that which gives shape to reality, at least in the world of living things. Perhaps what we call spirit is always connected to the material world, as the other side of one coin, and the soul has been the connector since the beginning of creation or since the "big bang".

In a very clearly presented argument, that expressly includes processes of the spirit and soul, physicist Thomas Görnitz, and psychologist Birgit Görnitz, have integrated conclusions from quantum information theory with a current understanding of brain and consciousness. A quotation from the cover blurb of their book: "Cosmically based, abstract quantum information provides the foundation for material and spirit. The evolution of the cosmos, of life and of consciousness can be viewed from a common viewpoint that reconciles our psychological experience with modern physics and biological knowledge, on a scientific basis." From C.F. von Weizsächer's idea of a "primal", the most abstract cosmic information that is thinkable, what is described here is a quantum physics path through to self-reflective consciousness. Step by step, the authors make clear how quantum information, with its laws that lie beyond our everyday experience, must be understood as a requirement for consciousness. But interpersonal and transpersonal psychic phenomena are also compatible with the laws of quantum physics. "Quantum information does not have to be limited to the body of the producer. Even when we have not yet got the wherewithal to work with such problems experimentally, and though there are reasons to believe that may never happen, the illustrated phenomenon of complex interconnections is nonetheless appropriate as a model. However, it must be clearly emphasised that this type of phenomena has nothing in common with the methods of traditional science. It is not an attempt to establish a cause and effect relationship, and as basically unique events, they lie outside the realm of what can be proven scientifically." (Görnitz and Görnitz, 2002)

I am mentioning these research trends here because they indicate that the phenomenon of representatives' awareness and participation in information outside the usual paths of communication, as well as processes of the soul in general, may very well correspond to the fundamentals of physics. At this point in time, quantum physics appears to be, at least principally, the most promising model, whether through the assumption of all-permeating and interconnecting quantum fields, or whether we look at the phenomena of widely distant parts interlaced into a whole. When interconnected parts become a whole, they need no energetic transference process to "know" about each other. If the processes of spirit and soul have a "real" basis inside the brain as well as outside the brain, then it is presumably based on the principles of matter, energy, and information, as they are made clear in quantum physics.

These comments are intended merely to put forth the idea that there may actually be a physical explanation for the often-astounding phenomenon of representative awareness, at least in principle. The possibility is worth considering, rather than simply dismissing what we see as hocus-pocus, purely suggestive behaviour, or some kind of group hysteria.

The practical importance of phenomena in constellations is not dependent on any scientific explanation or metaphor. Still, these and other ideas may open a way for clients and therapists to approach what is inexplicable in constellations, with an eye towards possible explanations in the future. The reverse is also true; the observable phenomena of representative awareness may encourage theorists and practitioners from other areas of psychology, sociology, or brain research to broaden their ideas about information processes in the psyche and interpersonal communication.

The Representatives

When we observe constellations carefully, a host of other important questions may arise. Do clients unconsciously choose representatives who fit into their family system? Many representatives are surprised when they are regularly chosen for very similar roles. When that happens, it does not skew the process of the constellation; in fact, it often deepens it because of the particular sensitivity of that representative. When additional representatives are needed after the initial configuration, the therapist often chooses representatives, more or less randomly, which does not seem to make any difference in the course of the constellation. It is true, however, that such questions have not really been objectively assessed.

To what extent are representatives in their roles free of their own experiences and prejudices? They aren't, but it does not seem to play any great part in what really happens. In general, most representatives react completely differently in different roles. Naturally, individuals are subject to their own emotional imprinting and their own repertoire of gestures. There are representatives who tend to initially close their eyes in every constellation, or drop to the floor, or something else. It is the therapist's task to look behind the form of the expression to the "accuracy" of the movements of the soul. It is very rare for a representative to act out a purely personal, theatrical performance that is unconnected to the energies of the constellation. Such a reaction would not find any resonance from the other representatives, unless the whole constellation got off track and developed its own dynamics, without relevance to the client and his or her family. In such a case, the therapist's experience and overview are of primary importance. These questions can only be addressed through very precise observation.

"Relative" Representation

Another area of difficulty lies in the fact that we use representatives not only for living persons but also for symptoms, secrets, war, death, aborted children, long-dead individuals, a profession, or a country. What can a person actually represent in a constellation and what exactly is it that is represented?

In the case of symptoms, illness or death, it is interesting that representatives sometimes react as if they were actually illness, symptoms or death. They react with an energy that is not entangled, like a reality that simply belongs to this person directly. Often, however, they react like an ill or deceased person in the family, that is, they respond in a way that is "entangled". This is another good reason for setting up symptoms or other abstract concepts, since they may well point to actual persons or events in the client's family system. But, what is being represented in the sense of "illness" or "war"? What can we know about the feelings of a three-month-old foetus? Can a person really capture the soul of an entire country?

Representation is not the substance of what is being represented. It communicates images and relationships at the level of the soul. One could say that the foetus "speaks" and "moves" in the soul of those who are living, or in the soul connections of the system. It is not America itself that is represented by a person; what appears is some particular aspect of a relationship to America, or the position America occupies in the group soul. Since missing people can also be felt, it is clear that what the representatives reveal is not the people or things themselves, but the relationships, processes in the soul, and the effects of events. Sometimes false connections emerge in constellations. For example, a representative feels a sense of certainty that this father is not his or her father. It may turn out that it was a grandfather who was actually the child of a different father, outside the family. What the son picks up in the present constellation as a feeling towards his father might possibly represent feelings that the grandfather actually felt in his family.

Constellations are sometimes like mythical stories, in which all realities speak like people in order to express core issues that would be difficult to portray and to experience in any other way. In the end, in order for constellations to have an effect, there must be some connection to reality in the representation, a clear, but not necessarily precise, connection with events and relationships in the soul.

Truth and Reality – The Phenomenological Method

What is the reality we deal with in constellations? How "true" is a constellation? Without getting into an extensive discussion of theories of knowledge, I would like to point out some of the fundamental assumptions in constellation work about reality, truth, and ways of knowing.

Reality is understood as the world of phenomena, the facts, but also our interpretation of them. Reality reveals itself through our consciousness, which is how we are able to relate to it. According to one's point of view, actual reality, that which acts, can be addressed in various ways. In constellations we observe the representatives, their movements, their words, their emotions, and their effects on the constellation, the client, the group and the therapist. We do not observe the actual family, who are usually present only in the person of the client, and then only in extremely complex soul connections. The reality of constellation work is the reality of a constellation.

How closely do these reflect the actual processes in a family? Objectively, the observer has only the process of a constellation as object, not the reality of the family. It would be very difficult to understand the phenomena in a constellation if there were no connection to the reality of the client's family, if it were merely by chance or imagined, or if it were a social construction of the constellation. Despite the current focus on subjective and social construction of information in theories of knowledge, the information has to relate to something. Family constellation work assumes that the world also exists independent of our consciousness and does not provide random or only "subjectively created" information. This world is clearly only reachable through personal experience, and we are well aware how strongly the object being observed is co-determined by the observer. You could describe the search for truth as a dialogical process, in which the observer and the observed reality each bring something separate, which then becomes interconnected through conscious awareness. In this conscious awareness, discrete events flow together with the constructs of meaning from our own understanding.

How are we to understand, then, a constellation's connection to reality? It is certainly not in the sense that constellations simply portray events and relationships in a family history in the manner of a documentary film (although some words and gestures do appear to be almost documentary, according to reports of clients). The concern here is not a precise congruence between objective reality and our words and understanding.

The truth in constellations is more easily compared to the truth of a theatre performance. Something is presented in image and word in a compressed form that allows us to experience a previously hidden reality. It is similar to truth in art. Art brings forth, in a concentrated form, what was previously invisible in reality.

Bert Hellinger, supported by Heidegger, referred to the old Greek term for truth, "*aletheia*", the revealed. In constellations, something is revealed of the realties of a relationship system or events. Something reveals itself, but only insofar as we can be aware of it within the limitations of our own consciousness. To use another metaphor, it is similar to a criminal case that needs to be solved. We look for events and connections of events that are not clear at the beginning, but are revealed through the representatives. The clues accumulate until the mystery is clear. In our case, therapists, somewhat melodramatically expressed, are more nearly detectives of love.

The approach to awareness in the face of complex realities is a phenomenological method. Phenomenology, in general, means developing awareness of reality as it appears and describing it. In the broader, philosophical sense, phenomenology is concerned with the nature of experience in the recognition of deeper structures in the available sensory information. In such recognition, the phenomena are one with "logos", or meaning.

To proceed in a phenomenological manner in a constellation, it is not sufficient to simply observe the phenomena. The deeper structures of the phenomena must be available to all attentive observers, and must make sense to them. That means that they can also be expressed in words, at least metaphorically. When we are dealing with issues of the soul, it is difficult to capture our phenomenological awareness in precise terminology (which is also reflected in the frequent use of inverted commas in this book). Phenomenological knowledge can often be expressed only in metaphor and vague language.

We depend on phenomenological insights in most social relationships, and often also in the initial stages of scientific investigation. If we observe, we have criteria and assumptions that serve as indicators in our exploration of reality. When we "real-ise" something, it is revealed to us in its entirety and we take it in. We may have a sudden inspiration, or are surprised by what appears, sometimes with a flash of recognition. Phenomenological awareness is open to the unexpected in the expected, and to that which "is startling or makes us sit up and take notice," (Bernhard Waldenfels). I once read in a crime novel, "Some ideas shoot through your brain like lightening, unprepared-for and unanticipated, with no prior associations" (Petros Makaris). This genre of literature seems to be a rich source of examples of phenomenological awareness.

What is revealed in constellations through the phenomenological method can only be verified by its correspondence to the facts of the family and its effect on the client and his or her family, and also in the fact that others, too, can suddenly see something that was previously unseen. We cannot do without this observation of phenomena, even though we know how vulnerable we are to imagination, incorrect interpretations and conclusions, crass associations, constructions, and mistakes. In constellation work, the therapist is constantly called upon to consciously hold his or her interpretation, actions, and assumptions in check so that a meaningful reality can reveal itself to the client. It demands diligence on the part of a therapist to be as fearless, as free of fantasies, and as free of judgement as possible, and to withhold any preconceived intention towards whatever might appear as the reality of the relationships.

The Systemic Method

In complex relationship systems, linear and cause-and-effect patterns are no longer adequate. This becomes clear the moment you sit in a marriage counselling session and listen to one partner and agree, and then you listen to the other and think that one is right, too. In psychosocial fields, there has long been the question of how to meaningfully intervene without getting caught in linear, causal thinking and speaking, and at the same time, to respect the structural organisation of living systems. How can we proceed systemically, with respect to the interrelationship of the parts organised and ordered within the whole in a way that makes the whole more than the sum of its parts and functions?

Family constellation work considers itself to be a systemic method in various ways. From the first moment, we look at the client in a context of fields of relationships with relevant persons, which may even reach across generations. There is scarcely another method that allows us to experience these reciprocal influences through time and space in a family in such a visible and compact form. In constellations, we can see relationship in action, to a certain extent. The term "entanglement" expresses the network of fates that occur, to a greater or lesser degree, more or less at the same time.

This systemic process is also integrated with an historical perspective to families. The here and now of a constellation, including the reciprocal effects of representatives, is related to the history and development of a family. Systems are enmeshed in the irreversible flow of time, and family histories and their effects in the soul are locked into a before and after in events and effects. To do justice to relationships, to understand their effects, and to have any influence, we have to connect linear and systemic thinking. If we were to symbolise linear thinking as a line and systemic thinking as a circle, we could visualise this connection in the form of a spiral. Language reflects these systemic movements through time in phrases such as, "the violence spiralled out of control". In the term "entanglement" we can see the more linear and energetic psychoanalytic concept of "repression", but we also see the image of circular networks of information and communication.

Family constellations are not a systemic method if we are refering to a "systemic" approach to circular processes, cause and effect, processes of communication in families that reach no conclusions. In constellations, the structure of communication in a family is not what is in question, and the representatives actually communicate very little verbally. What remains in the foreground is not this circular communication, but the entanglements. Systemic processes are more evident in the form of a shared participation of knowledge in social fields than in the form of communicative processes. System and soul are on the same level to a certain extent.

In a broader sense, constellations can be described as systemic because they function as a metaphorical process. Insofar as systems cannot be described in terms of causal links and complexities, they can only be portrayed in metaphorical language, stories, and pictures. In a picture we can simultaneously take in the totality of information and processes as a complete whole. In this sense, we always function systemically (not in reflection and thought). Sometimes it takes only a picture in a children's book to make us remember a particular fairy tale. The picture has stored the essential information about the whole story and a glance at it transmits the events that began the story, the theme that holds it together, and the end that resolves everything.

A family picture in a constellation also depicts a history, but without the usual analysis of linear-causal relationship processes. Sentences of bonds and resolution are usually very general and metaphoric, not in a formulation of causal connections, but in a way that makes the interconnections comprehensible. For example, if there seems to be a possible connection between a woman's difficulty getting pregnant and her grandfather's loss of his first wife in childbirth, there are sentences that could indicate that connection. "Dear Grandpa, when I see how much pain it caused you to lose your first wife, I also hold back from having a child." Or, "Please be friendly towards me if I find the courage to have a child, even though you lost your first wife and child during the baby's birth." Sentences like these are often not logical, but are formulated in relation to the unconscious processes of the client and his or her family. Statements of causality are more likely to tempt the client into thinking of movements that will solve the problem and put an end to it without loosening the network of influence from the individual parts. In constellations, causal statements do not serve to explain events, but rather state reasons for the connections. The reason and the effect are seen, or sometimes stated, with no explanation of the individual connections.

The development of constellations has moved increasingly in the direction of less verbalisation, and more trust in what can be seen. The systemic dynamic is then not constrained or obscured by words, but allowed to resonate in an image in the soul. Nonetheless, some explanatory statements from representatives or the therapist may be needed when the pictures are not clear enough to be taken in. A drawback of metaphorical systemic work is that it sometimes remains vague, but this is, at the same time, also one of the strong points of the work. The client's soul is open and free to find the "rightness" or "truth" with a view to future action.

Helping

Family constellations are not psychotherapy in the usual sense of the word, although the method may be used within the framework of psychotherapy. The intent of psychotherapy is healing and it is aimed at resolving personality disorders and specifically defined psychological, psychosomatic, traumatic and psychiatric illness. The client, or patient, remains in this process until symptoms have been resolved, until there is some improvement or healing, or until it is clear that a psychotherapeutic approach can be of no further help. Depending upon the training and licence of the therapist, any of this may also occur in family constellations as an indirect result, but it is not the primary goal.

Constellations are a tool for increasing awareness. In the way of a prophecy or a wise pronouncement, they simply bring to light the inter-connections of fate and their effects on our lives. They help to make the reality of a particular life visible and, when possible, to allow love to flow, but without trying to influence what the client chooses to do with this life. Constellation leaders rarely work long-term their clients. They do not intervene in their clients' lives by assigning tasks for change or evaluating their success or failure (although, of course, some therapists who do constellations may choose to do this). Constellations offer liberating insight into the turns of fate that have occurred up to this point in time, they bring relationships into order in a healing and growth-supporting way, and they lend strength as individuals learn to accept the lives of their parents and ancestors. There is basic trust in people's competence and responsibility and their ability to deal well with whatever has happened.

This is a view of help that differs from many other therapeutic approaches. Although we often confront very difficult fates, this kind of helping without trying to influence outcomes seems light. One can feel accepted within one's family and life, and experience a firm foundation of love. Changes do occur, but not because we try to make them happen. There is respect for one's own responsibility, and no justify anything to others. There is no involvement in a therapeutic relationship or in formalised, structured psychotherapy. These attitudes are valuable and useful to many people.

For those who would be helpers, it means looking at helping in a different way. Only those who have accepted their own families and their own lives have any help to offer. It means relinquishing the temptation to give someone more than they need or can use. Help has to suit the circumstances of the client's life and fate, as well as personal conditions, abilities and decisions. Where, when, and how supportive intervention is possible is determined by a basic respect for the client's dignity.

A helper, of course, needs skills to be prepared for whatever comes. If the helper has unresolved needs, he or she may end up drawing strength from a well of compassion for the weak and for the victims. A helper's family pattern of being the "competent one" or the "rescuer" can lead to an illusion of being able to handle any fate of any client, and doing it better than the person's own parents. Real help, however, does not come from the therapist as a person; it is carried by the strength and the wisdom of the client's family soul and by those greater forces that are so difficult to name. In this sense, family constellations help the helpers as well.

Psychotherapy, Counselling, Support in Life Crises, and Applied Philosophy?

Bert Hellinger has continued to explore the further development of family constellations. Some of the newer directions have stimulated much discussion, such as "movements of the soul" and a change in the view of victims and perpetrators, (for example, perpetrators are no longer excluded from the constellation, that is, the system). Despite criticism of some recent developments, we should not overlook the basic continuity that runs through the entire background and development. The later, sometimes radically different movements do not exclude earlier methods. As a result, there is a wider range of procedures, ways of understanding, and therapeutic and philosophical attitudes that have crystallised in the helping fields.

This work developed first as a form of psychotherapy and continues to be a practical application in that field. Many suffering from physical or mental illness are turning to family constellations in search of relief and healing. The therapists looking for paths to healing come from a wide variety of psychotherapeutic approaches. They use constellations to identify a client's essential problems and to look for possible resolution, for example, by dissolving a bond of identification with another family member. Marriage and family counsellors are using constellations to find a helpful orientation for marital or family difficulties.

Experience has indicated that representatives in a constellation are strongly connected to a "soul field" that extends even beyond the family. This makes their reactions useful and meaningful for finding solutions that might be beyond the knowledge and capacities of the actual family. A new element that has brought fresh insight and often surprising solutions is the procedure of allowing the representatives freedom of movement, assisted by minimal interventions from the therapist. Constellations touch forces of fate, in the face of which even the therapist is small and ignorant. We sometimes reach our own limits and are confronted with solutions that perhaps go against what we might personally consider a good direction. For example, a perpetrator might be drawn towards his or her victims in death, in the sure knowledge that only death can end what life cannot heal, and this is the only movement that will bring peace. The family soul appears in the context of an even larger field, and the constellation changes from psychotherapy, family therapy or counselling to a process of "accompanying the soul" (Bert Hellinger), a process that connects us to the movements of the soul in a greater, incomprehensible process. The therapist suddenly stands in service to the care of the soul, or a kind of support for living, or a more comprehensive kind of spiritual guidance.

Finally, there is one more element that has come into Bert Hellinger's most recent work, which he calls "moving with the spirit".

Classical family constellations and the movements of the soul are orientated towards feelings, including everything we can be aware of through feelings, and what we feel that can move us. In this new variant, the therapist and client look towards "the spirit". In spirit, we are able to transcend sensory reality and our experience of good and evil and move beyond the arena of what is bad or what is not in order. Here, the therapist accompanies the client on a more philosophical path. In Hellinger's words:

"I will illustrate this with an example. A client has many complaints about his or her parents, or has negative feelings about the bad things he or she lived through in childhood. We used to feel sympathy with such clients and think, 'I can help this person.' If I think philosophically, though, nothing that comes from the spirit is bad, that is impossible. If there is a creative force behind everything, there is nothing that can resist it. So, now I look at the situation philosophically and demand that the client look at the situation in the same way. Whatever has happened, he or she says, 'Thank you. I will take strength from this. I take these parents as special people who have given me a special strength that is essential for my life.' Suddenly, everything that has happened is transformed. It becomes precious." (Bert Hellinger in a lecture in Garmisch-Partenkirchen, February 2004)

A family constellation at this level is no longer a family constellation and orientates the soul processes and bonds towards the spirit. "The spirit is light. Whoever is transformed in the spirit is light of foot. The spirit burdens the earth very little; and burdens a person very little; and is pleased in the face of everything that is. Moving with the spirit makes everything simple." (Bert Hellinger)

In this view, are constellations leaving their grounding in psychotherapy, counselling, and personal development? Does this mean that only a therapist who is advanced in the philosophical sense, or "enlightened" can travel this path? If that were true, then we could also add, "after enlightenment comes cleaning the floor". Or, taking a biblical image, Jesus allows the apostles a brief, transforming glimpse on Mount Tabor, before he takes them back down into everyday life, with all its horror and despair. Whatever philosophical judgements this may elicit, the value of Bert Hellinger's move to an applied philosophy does not lie in changing family constellations into a spiritual experience, rendering the work as a therapeutic method superfluous. The gain lies in an attitude and spirit that deepens and broadens the usual concept of help in various social areas, firmly anchored in the processes of bonding and resolution in the soul. Perhaps we can paraphrase Bert Hellinger's words about man and woman, and say that the soul follows the spirit, and the spirit serves the soul.

The critical question remains: how can we overcome traumatic experiences that often have effects over generations, our own or of others, in a way that eases and reconciles? How can this be remembered in a way that it can also be forgotten without repressing it, at a personal or societal level? How can it be forgotten so that we are open to future love and growth? Using the word "precious" in view of the enormous suffering of man pushes us to the outermost spiritual boundaries. Mystics of all religions and the "eternal philosophy" (Aldous Huxley) have always come close. As a therapist, one can only dare to think these philosophical, spiritual, or mystic-religious thoughts when looking simply at their healing effects in the fate of one individual. This worldview, in which all that happens is held in universal growth and all-inclusive love, needs to be connected to what an individual person can take in and what actually helps. It is possible to maintain such a view when we see how often people do come through suffering with courage, strength and acceptance, and go on to live fulfilled lives. On the other hand, it poses questions and challenges when we actually feel the terrible suffering and infliction of pain.

In the multiplicity of methods and helping fields, family constellation work will only be able to find its place with an "applied philosophy", if it stays in close contact to people's suffering in the soul, and if "orders of the spirit" remain closely connected to the processes of bonding and resolution in the soul and in relationships. In this way, it can contribute to an integration of psychotherapy, counselling, care of the soul, and spirituality and offer a more holistic approach to helping in situations where specific therapies are not sufficient. Family constellation work, wide open to all the workings of the soul, is a support to life itself.

Bibliography

A selection of readings in family constellations and other related material mentioned in this book.

De Philipp, W. (2006): Systemaufstellungen im Einzelsetting. Heidelberg (Carl-Auer).

Franke U. (2003): In My Mind's Eye. Family Constellations in Individual Therapy and Counselling. Heidelberg (Carl-Auer).

Franke-Gricksch, M. (2003): You're One of Us. Systemic Insights and Solutions for Teachers, Students and Parents. Heidelberg (Carl-Auer).

Görnitz T. u. B. (2002): Der kreative Kosmos, Geist und Materie aus Information. Heidelberg (Spektrum).

Heidegger, M. (1989): Überlieferte Sprache und technische Sprache. St. Gallen (Erker).

Hellinger, B. (1994): Ordnungen der Liebe. Ein Kursbuch. Heidelberg (Carl-Auer), 7th edition 2000.

Hellinger B., G. Weber, H. Beaumomt (1998): Love's Hidden Symmetry. What Makes Love Work in Relationships. Phoenix, AZ (Zeig, Tucker & Theisen).

Hellinger B., G. ten Hövel (1999): Acknowledging What Is. Heidelberg (Carl-Auer).

Hellinger B. (2001a): Einsicht durch Verzicht. Der phänomenologische Erkenntnisweg in der Psychotherapie am Beispiel des Familienstellens. In Weber, G. (ed.): Derselbe Wind läßt viele Drachen steigen. Systemische Lösungen im Einklang. Heidelberg (Carl-Auer), pp.14–28.

Hellinger, B. (2001b): Entlassen werden wir vollendet. Späte Texte. München (Kösel).

Hellinger, B. (2002): Insights. Lectures and Stories. Heidelberg (Carl-Auer).

Hellinger, B. (2006): No Waves Without the Ocean. Heidelberg (Carl-Auer).

Hellinger, B. a. H. Beaumont (2002): Touching Love. A Teaching Seminar with Bert Hellinger and Hunter Beaumont. Phoenix, AZ (Zeig, Tucker & Theisen).

Hellinger, B. (2003): To the Heart of the Matter. Brief Therapies. Heidelberg (Carl-Auer).

Hellinger, B. (2003): Farewell. Family Constellations with Descendants of Victims and Perpetraters. Phoenix, AZ (Zeig, Tucker & Theisen).

Hellinger, B. (2003): Ordnungen des Helfens. Ein Schulungsbuch. 2 volumes. Heidelberg (Carl-Auer).

Höppner, G. (2001): Heilt Demut – wo Schicksal wirkt? Eine Studie zu Effekten des Familien-Stellens nach Bert Hellinger. Munich (Profil).

Hohnen, H. a. B. Ulsamer (eds.) (2001): Bert Hellinger: Mit der Seele gehen. Freiburg (Herder).

König, O. (2004): Familienwelten. Theorie und Praxis von Familienaufstellungen. Stuttgart (Klett-Cotta).

Kutschera, I. a. Ch. Schäffler (2006): What's Out of Order Here? Illness and Family Constellations. Heidelberg (Carl-Auer).

Laszlo, E. (1996): The Whispering Pond. Rockport, MA (Element Books).

Mahr, A. (1998b): Die Weisheit kommt nicht zu den Faulen. Von Geführtwerden und von der Technik in Familienaufstellungen. In: G. Weber (ed.): Praxis des Familien-Stellens. Heidelberg (Carl-Auer).

Mahr, A. (2001): Die Offenheit des wissenden Feldes. Von personalen zu transpersonalen Erfahrungen. In: G. Weber (ed.): Derselbe Wind läßt viele Drachen steigen. Systemische Lösungen im Einklang. Heidelberg (Carl-Auer).

McTaggert, L. (2001): The Field. London (Harper Collins).

Nelles, W. (2002): Liebe, die löst. Einsichten aus dem Familienstellen. Heidelberg (Carl-Auer).

Nelles, W. (2003): Das Hellinger-Prinzip. Informationen und Klärungen. Freiburg (Herder).

Neuhauser, J. (2001): Supporting Love. How Love Works in Couple Relationships. Bert Hellinger's Work with Couples. Heidelberg (Carl-Auer).

Praxis der Systemaufstellung. Beiträge zu Lösungen in Familien und Organisationen. Munich (Deutsche Gesellschaft für Systemaufstellungen).

Ruppert, F. (2002): Verwirrte Seelen. Der verborgene Sinn von Psychosen. Grundzüge einer systemischen Psychotraumatologie. Munich (Kösel).

Ruppert, F. (2005): Trauma, Bindung und Familienstellen. Seelische Verletzungen verstehen und heilen. Stuttgart (Kett-Cotta).

Schäfer, T. (1998): Was die Seele krank macht und was sie heilt. Die psychotherapeutische Arbeit Bert Hellingers. Munich (Knaur).

Schäfer, T. (2004): Wenn der Körper Signale gibt. Wege aus der Krankheit durch Systemische Aufstellungen. Munich (Knaur).

Schlötter, P. (2005): Vertraute Sprache und ihre Entdeckung. Systemaufstellungen sind kein Zufallsprodukt. Der empirische Nachweis. Heidelberg (Carl-Auer).

Schneider, J. R. (1998a): Familienaufstellungen mit Einzelklienten mit Hilfe von Figuren. In: G. Weber (ed.): Praxis des Familienstellens. Heidelberg (Carl-Auer), pp. 182–193.

Schneider, J. R (1998b): Supervision mit Hilfe von Aufstellungen. In: G. Weber (ed.): Praxis des Familien-Stellens. Heidelberg (Carl-Auer), pp. 366–376.

Schneider, J. R. (2001b): Zur Technik des Familien-Stellens. In: G. Weber (ed.): Derselbe Wind läßt viele Drachen steigen. Systemische Lösungen im Einklang. Heidelberg (Carl-Auer), pp. 349–388.

Schneider, J. R. a. B. Gross (2000): Ach wie gut, dass ich es weiß. Märchen und andere Geschichten in der systemisch-phänomenologischen Therapie. Heidelberg (Carl-Auer).

Sheldrake, R. (2003): The Sense of Being Stared at and Other Aspects of the Extended Mind. New York (Crown).

Sparrer, I. (2002): Wunder, Lösung und System. Lösungsfokussierte systemische Strukturaufstellungen für Therapie und Organisationsberatung. Heidelberg (Carl-Auer), 4ᵗʰ ed. 2006.

Ulsamer, B. a. T. Breyfolgle (2005): The Healing Power of the Past. The Systemic Therapy of Bert Hellinger. Nevada City, CA (Underwood).

Ulsamer, B. (2003): The Art and Practise of Family Constellations. Leading Family Constellations as Developed by Bert Hellinger. Heidelberg (Carl-Auer).

Ulsamer, B. a. M. Hell (2003): Wie hilft Familien-Stellen? Münsterschwarzach-Abtei (Vier-Türme-Verlag).

Varga v. Kibed, M. u. I. Sparrer (2003): Ganz im Gegenteil. Tetralemmaarbeit und andere Grundformen systemischer Strukturaufstellungen. Heidelberg (Carl-Auer), 4ᵗʰ ed.

Weber, G. (2000): Die Praxis der Organisationsaufstellungen. Basics und Besonderes. In: G. Weber (ed.): Praxis der Organisationsaufstellungen. Heidelberg (Carl-Auer), 2ⁿᵈ ed. 2002, pp. 34–90.

Weber, G. (ed.) (2001): Derselbe Wind läßt viele Drachen steigen. Systemische Lösungen im Einklang. Heidelberg (Carl-Auer).

Weber-Schäfer, P. (ed.) (1982): Zen. Aussprüche und Verse der Zenmeister. Frankfurt (Insel).

Zeilinger, A. (2003): Einsteins Schleier. Die neue Welt der Quantenphysik. Munich (Beck).

About the Author

 *Jakob Robert Schneider* studied philosophy, theology, physical education and pedagogy. He has a private practice for counselling and group therapy, and gives family constellation seminars in Germany and abroad. He is an active member of the *International Arbeitsgemeinschaft systemische Lösungen nach Bert Hellinger* (IAG) [the international association for family constellation work] and is founding editor of the German journal *Praxis der Systemaufstellung*.